Greece & Rome

NEW SURVEYS IN THE CLASSICS No. 27

LATIN HISTORIANS

BY

C. S. KRAUS & A. J. WOODMAN

Published for the Classical Association

OXFORD UNIVERSITY PRESS

1997

Oxford University Press, Great Clarendon Street, Oxford OX2 6DP
Oxford New York
Athens Auckland Bangkok Bogata Bombay
Buenos Aires Calcutta Cape Town Dar es Salaam
Delhi Florence Hong Kong Istanbul Karachi
Kuala Lumpur Madras Madrid Melbourne
Mexico City Nairobi Paris Singapore
Taipei Tokyo Toronto
and associated companies in
Berlin Ibadan

ISSN 0017–3835
ISBN 0–19 922293–2
© Oxford University Press, 1997

Printed in Great Britain
by Bell and Bain Ltd.,
Glasgow

PREFACE

Our principal aim in this booklet has been to write essays on three major Latin historians which we hope will stimulate interest. Our intention has not been to supersede previous *Greece & Rome* booklets on Livy (by P. G. Walsh, 1974) and Tacitus (by F. R. D. Goodyear, 1970): we have not been concerned primarily with introducing readers to 'the state of the question', although we have referred to recent research and have tried to cover some of the main issues. In an Appendix we have assembled, for the sake of convenience, some basic bibliographical information on the authors and topics we have discussed.

The Introduction was written collaboratively; Chapter 2 was shared (the section on the *BC* is by AJW, the others by CSK); Chapter 3 is by CSK, Chapters 4 and 5 by AJW. CSK would like to thank Jane Chaplin and John Rich for their comments, together with the participants in the literature seminar, held at the Institute of Classical Studies in spring 1995, for reactions to her interpretation of the *BJ*; AJW would like to thank Ronald Martin, Stephen Oakley, and Robin Seager. We both owe a special debt of gratitude to David Levene.

C. S. Kraus
September 1996   A. J. Woodman

CONTENTS

I. INTRODUCTION

The word 'history' is ambiguous: it can refer both to events and to the account of events as written by a historian. Historians may be eye-witnesses of the events which they describe; more often they rely on sources in the form of text, whether written or oral (stories, inscriptions, documents, the accounts of other historians). Thus writing history, for which the term 'historiography' is often used, generally involves the act of reading as well as that of interpretation. Yet 'historiography' is itself an ambiguous term, since it may also denote the study both of the historian's written work and, more generally, of the theory and history of historical writing. These various overlaps of terminology underline the fact, which scholars have come increasingly to realize, that in practice it is very difficult to separate the 'history' of a given period (i.e. the events, the things that happened) from its 'historiography' (i.e. the texts in which those events are (re)told and analysed), a difficulty which in its turn gives rise to various further problems.

Original events[1] no longer exist, except insofar as they leave traces, either physical (a temple, a coin, an aqueduct) or literary, in the form of texts written either soon afterwards (a commemorative inscription, the text of a law) or long after (the history of the early Roman republic written several centuries later by a middle-republican historian).[2] It is from these traces that modern historians construct their stories about what happened in the ancient world. And these stories are essentially no more than possible models of a vanished world, whether they take the form of what may be called analytical history (the study of a particular topic or period from one of a number of different viewpoints, concentrating on e.g. economic or social or cultural aspects) or narrative history (retelling the history of a given period or people in story form, using conventions similar to those of a traditional novel). But texts, be they ancient or modern, are slippery things, both physically (crucial ancient texts may be lacunose, corrupt, or exist only as a paraphrase by a later author) and philosophically (the meaning of words is not fixed, and any given text will be interpreted differently by different generations of readers).[3] Even if we believe (and not all scholars do) that with care we can come close to knowing how an original audience might have understood an ancient text, we are still left with the fact that that text is not a piece of plate glass through which to view the ancient world but is only one version of that world, one writer's interpretation, now filtered through centuries of copying, scholarly attention, and our own expectations, levels of knowledge, and ways of reading.

Because so much of the evidence for vanished events is itself contestable, and because any story that a historian writes itself forms a text that may later be used to construct a new model of these vanished events, the *form* of a text can contribute as much to its meaning as does its content. And if under 'form' we include such intangible elements as the political context in which the text was written, the likely bias of the author (though, as we shall see, this is often a matter of continuing debate), the literary expectations of any original audience, and finally the norms and codes of the genre of history-writing itself, then it becomes clear that the *way* a story is told is as important as (indeed, is part of) the story itself.[4] The situation outlined generally here obtains for anyone trying to read or reconstruct the history of ancient Rome: as T. J. Cornell points out in his new and monumental history of early Rome, 'The most important evidence for the early history of Rome comes from literary sources.'[5]

If the history and historiography of Rome are thus interdependent, it is clearly of great importance to know how the Romans wrote their history. A historian such as Livy, who lived several centuries after many of the events which he purports to describe, relied on a succession of earlier historians writing in both Latin and Greek: Fabius Pictor, Gaius Acilius, Postumius Albinus, the elder Cato, Polybius, Cassius Hemina, Calpurnius Piso, Gaius Fannius, Gnaeus Gellius, Coelius Antipater, Sempronius Asellio, Claudius Quadrigarius, Valerius Antias, Cornelius Sisenna, Licinius Macer, Aelius Tubero, Asinius Pollio, and Sallust.[6] Not all wrote the same kind of history. Among them they represent two different types: (i) history of a relatively short, well-defined period (often a war), such as that of Coelius (on the second Punic war) or of Sisenna (on the Social war and after) and (ii) history of Rome from its founding (history *ab urbe condita* or *a Remo et Romulo*), such as the annals of Antias and Macer. There was also a third type, universal history, which treated all parts of the inhabited world (the *oikoumene*); since Roman history was at heart local history, this genre developed late at Rome, though Polybius (whose work covers the period 220–146 B.C.) thought of himself as a universal historian (see also below, p. 54).[7] Nearly all of this work either is lost or survives only in fragmentary form; we do know, however, that the careers of these writers cover the period from (roughly) 200 B.C. to 35 B.C. But, since the traditional date for the foundation of Rome is the mid-eighth century B.C., we are left with an interval of over five hundred years during which no history was written in Rome at all. Where, then, did the earliest historians derive their information for the earliest centuries of Rome?

The traditional story of how history grew at Rome is that told by Cicero and elaborated by later critics: it is a dismal tale of plain, unadorned, thin narratives, a mere 'compilation of chronicles' (Cic. *De orat.* 2.52 *annalium confectio*) even up through the orator's own lifetime (he imagines his friend Atticus begging him to remedy the situation by writing history himself: *Leg.* 1.5–9, cf. also *Att.* 16.13.2).[8] According to this picture, Roman history began with the (lost) *Annales maximi*, a year-by-year chronicle that is said to have been posted for public view on white boards (*tabulae dealbatae*), later codified in some form, perhaps as a large inscription, and maintained by the *pontifex maximus* (high priest). It is said to have dated back (perhaps) to the fifth century B.C.[9] and to have contained the names of annual magistrates and other officials, and notices of famines and eclipses and of primarily ritual material.[10] Yet, even if the earliest historians had access to a record which pre-dated themselves by so long a time, there still remains a period of about three centuries from the founding of the city for which no information other than some form of traditional memory was available, but which Livy nevertheless took four books (more than 300 pages of Oxford Text) to describe.[11]

Nor should we be optimistic about the reliability either of the information transmitted by the *Annales maximi* or of the use which historians may have made of its information. A recent investigator of the *Annales* concludes as follows:[12]

We ought, I think, to envision the pontifical chronicle as a gigantic, poorly formatted, difficult to read, inscription on bronze, probably consisting of several individual bronze *tabulae* ['plates'] incised by a variety of hands, which may well have been awkwardly positioned, and perhaps, in the later stages of its life, even plagued with gaps. At some point, it is quite possible that some sort of restoration was carried out, which may have adulterated the original records. One visualizes a conscientious consulting historian, standing before this mass of data, with wax tablet in hand. As he reads on, he finds that it is loaded with uninteresting prodigies, famines, eclipses and the like, all listed under eponymous magistrates. Eventually, perhaps, he gives up in disgust . . .: as the more interesting (and certainly more easily and comfortably consulted) accounts of the first annalists (who had been forced to consult the chronicle) became available, people ceased standing in the elements craning their necks to read a lot of banal entries.

Two points in this conclusion deserve emphasis. The first is the 'uninteresting' and 'banal' nature of the record, which in both content and form is far removed from even the minimum requirements of narrative history.[13] The second is the extreme difficulty of consulting the record. The consensus of modern research is that the Romans had a persistent disregard for the retrieval of information,[14] which no doubt explains the commonly accepted view that 'Roman historians did not, as a general rule, carry out original research.'[15] As far as we can tell, in fact, from the very beginning historians of early Rome primarily used other written histories as sources, modelling their own work on, and polemically engaging with, their precursors' in ways generally familiar to us from the work of poets (see below, p. 48 n. 110). The earliest Roman historian, Fabius Pictor, who wrote in Greek, looked, as Cornell has remarked, to the canons and methods of Greek historiography, using Greek accounts of early Rome as his source;[16] later writers reacted both to Greek historians and, once Cato the Elder had invented a prose style for Latin and written history in it, to the growing prose tradition in their own language.

Roman historians did on occasion consult the research of others, conveniently grouped under the general heading of 'antiquarians'.[17] Even here, however, it does not follow that their methods were the same as ours: for instance, Livy famously refers to 'sources' (*auctores*) in the plural when he means a single source; and it has been argued that many other 'scholarly' conventions of historiographical narrative are purely mendacious.[18] What is more, as Cicero and Livy knew, antiquarian genealogical research was itself often characterized by distortion and free invention (Cic. *Brut.* 62, Livy 8.40.4–5). Finally, none of these possible sources for early Roman history provided more than a barebones structure, nothing like the elaborate narratives we find in Livy and others.[19] It is certainly true that by the time Fabius Pictor wrote, the Romans had a 'highly developed sense of their past', and it has been argued that the remarkably coherent account of early Roman history found in the extant sources can only be explained as relying on the 'collective, and accepted, oral memory of the nation': that is, oral tradition and the fierce Roman sense of identity themselves constitute an important source for early Rome.[20] As Cornell has reminded us, however, this sense of the past is not unproblematic: 'the historical tradition of the Roman Republic was not an authenticated official record or an objective critical reconstruction; rather, it was an ideological construct designed to control, to justify, and to inspire.'[21] So, although the problem of the content and form of the *Annales* did not arise for authors writing the history of their own time, the fact that ancient historians were not researchers, the often problematic status of the research which they sometimes consulted, and the markedly nationalistic and ideological nature of the tradition in which they lived and worked have profound implications for our understanding of the kind of literature they produced.

It is fairly safe to assume, however, that until about twenty years ago, the fundamental differences between ancient and modern historians, especially with regard to their respective assumptions about the truth value of their narratives, were largely ignored. A classic example is provided by Cicero's dialogue *De oratore* ('On the orator'), produced in 55 B.C. but set in 91. Cicero, surveying the early Roman historians (2.51–4), found them deficient when compared with their Greek predecessors and he therefore set out the methods by which 'proper' history should be written (2.62–4). Everyone accepts that Cicero's passage provides crucial evidence for the nature of Roman historiography, and, when discussing it in 1979, the distinguished Oxford historian P.A. Brunt concluded as follows:[22] 'Cicero is not expressly advocating a type of historical exposition different from that commonly employed by modern political historians.' Such an attitude was entirely typical of its time: in studies such as those of S. Usher (1969) or M. Grant (1970) or C. W. Fornara (1983) it was stated or implied that 'history has altered but little' over the course of time.[23] And the same attitude underlies what modern historians themselves wrote about the history of the Roman republic and empire.

In the same year as Brunt's statement appeared, however, T. P. Wiseman published *Clio's Cosmetics*, a book which has since become a landmark in the study of the Roman historians. Wiseman argued that the Romans practised (in our terms) 'unhistorical thinking', that their historians were profoundly different from ours in that they assimilated historiography to poetry and oratory, and in particular that the early Roman historians (upon whom the later ones were so dependent) resorted to invention on a large scale. If we compare the paucity and unreliability of the evidence for early Roman history with the scale of Livy's work (above, p. 3), Wiseman's conclusions seem not only reasonable but almost inevitable; yet so disquieting an argument could not fail to provoke a reaction. In 1982, while acknowledging that the book 'raised important and challenging questions', Cornell offered an extended critique and explicitly gave his support to Brunt and the traditional view.[24] But Wiseman stuck to his guns and, although Cornell returned to the issue in 1986 and afterwards, has maintained his position in his subsequent writing.[25]

In 1988 the traditional view as elaborated by Brunt was confronted directly by A. J. Woodman in his book, *Rhetoric in Classical Historiography*. He argued that, when Roman historians in their prefaces profess to be telling the 'truth', they are denying bias and not (in our terms) 'fabrication'; and he provided a systematic analysis of *De oratore* 2.62–4 which showed that Cicero was recommending for historiography the oratorical techniques, including *inuentio* ('invention'), which were advocated in rhetorical handbooks.[26] Although Woodman's book too enjoyed something of a mixed reception, its detailed exposition of ancient historiographical theory corroborated Wiseman's hypothesis and ensured that the debate on the nature of Roman historical writing continued.[27]

Yet this debate has been conducted largely in the pages and footnotes of scholarly monographs and academic periodicals, with only a severely restricted impact, if any, on material which is readily accessible to teachers and students in schools.[28] The present book is not the place to repeat arguments which have already been made elsewhere; but it is of great importance that readers should be aware that the very nature of Roman historiography has been subjected to severe questioning and that the debate continues. In the following discussions of Sallust, Livy, Tacitus, and others it is taken for granted that the views broadly associated with Wiseman and Woodman are correct. It is also taken for granted that since these ancient texts are as much literary as historical, a literary approach, in which one reads for structure, style, and theme (among other things), can offer new insights into the way these historians saw their past and their present, and indeed into the use which we today can make of their work.

Finally, as a sort of postscript, we turn to a brief consideration of what, if anything, can be said about the now fragmentary work of the early historians. From the often exiguous remains we can sometimes see points of contact (and of difference) with extant texts. The best-known examples of overlap concern Piso's story of the aedile Gnaeus Flavius (27P, also told by Livy at 9.46) and Quadrigarius' story of Manlius Torquatus' single combat with a fourth-century Gaul (10[b]P, also told by Livy at 7.9.6–10.14): the comparison of the latter pair is the textbook analysis of stylistic development found in many discussions of Latin prose style.[29] Many of the fragments show that the earlier historians shared concerns with the later; indeed, these early writers, working with native Roman or Italian traditions and with the great texts of Greek historiography, defined the parameters and questions with which their genre would concern itself. These are then taken up, challenged, and modified by later authors, who nevertheless keep quite close to the general outlines of the field as laid out by their precursors. Primary among those concerns are questions of self-definition, firstly of the historian: what form is his history to take, annals or monograph or an account of the foundation of cities? what items is he to include, and what to avoid? of what value is his own experience in politics or war? and of what value is the work he is producing? Roman culture put considerable pressure on intellectuals in all fields to show that their work had practical justification and application; for literature to be taken seriously, it had to be useful. Of what use was the story of Rome?

Secondly, these historians addressed the question of the self-definition of Rome itself. The history of Rome was essentially the history of one city which grew in 1000 years to include within its boundaries most of the known world: the resulting influx of foreign peoples, languages, and ideas, already an issue by the middle Republic, posed problems of self-identity. What did it mean to be Roman?[30] A more specific concern, especially from the perspective of the earliest historians, who were to a man engaged in politics and the military, was public life and the *res publica*: the relations between the ruling élite and the populace, and the shifting boundaries of the ruling class, which like the empire it controlled gradually grew to encompass more and more outsiders, were of paramount importance. Politics and the military continued to hold centre stage, though, as the empire grew, individual actors became increasingly important: these powerful new leaders can be seen emerging already in earlier historiography, but especially in Sallust, Livy, and of course under the Empire, in Tacitus.[31] Whatever the focus, however, the structure of the state itself was always visible, as the historians reported – with varying degrees of emphasis or belief – religious ritual and prodigies, the annual change of magistracies, the diplomatic interaction between Rome and its allies or enemies, the development or change of institutions, the passing of laws and decrees. It is in these passages, with their often simple, list format and reporting of information basic to the functioning of the state, that the 'origins' of Latin historio-graphy, the *Annales maximi*, make their spirit, if not their actual influence, felt.[32] In what follows, we will trace many of these themes and questions as they were elaborated in the historians whose work survives.

NOTES

1. On the problematic notion of 'event' see e.g. P. Veyne, *Writing History* (Manchester, 1984) s.vv. 'events' and 'facts' (Index) and L.O. Mink, *Historical Understanding* (Ithaca, 1987) s.v. 'event' (Index). On sources as texts which reflect reality only indirectly, see e.g. Veyne, 4–5 'in no case is what historians call an event grasped directly and fully; it is always grasped incompletely and laterally, through documents and statements, let us say through *tekmeria*, traces, impressions . . . Of the text of man, the historian knows the variations but never the text itself.' It is possible to take the further step of asserting that there are no past events beyond texts: that all history is in fact only events under a description.

2. Given our concern exclusively with texts, we have consciously ignored archaeological remains in our discussion. Such remains can confirm or challenge the historical model built from textual sources; it is worth noting, however, that archaeological data mean nothing *by themselves*: they too must be contextualized and interpreted. For examples of that process see M. Beard and J. Henderson, *Classics: A Very Short Introduction* (Oxford, 1995).

3. For an introduction to modern critical approaches such as 'reader-response' theory and their application to the classics see the essays and suggestions for further reading in de Jong-Sullivan (1994); for an introduction to the chief concepts of literary criticism see F. Lentricchia and T. McLaughlin, edd., *Critical Terms for Literary Study* (Chicago, 1990).

4. On the distinction between the story and the way it is told see S. Chatman, *Story and Discourse* (Ithaca, 1978); on historical narrative, in addition to the items cited in nn. 1 above and 13 below, see H. White, *Metahistory* (Baltimore, 1973). The fundamental texts for the discipline of narratology (the study of how stories work) are G. Genette, *Narrative Discourse: an Essay in Method* (Ithaca, 1980) and M. Bal, *Narratology* (Toronto, 1985); others are listed in the General Bibliography to de Jong-Sullivan (1994), 282–3.

5. Cornell (1995), 1–2.

6. For more on the early historians see bibliographical Appendix; for Livy's sources see Oakley (1997), 13–20.

7. Livy's annalistic history of Rome from its founding will have become universal in its later books (now lost) as Rome conquered the *oikoumene*; other representatives of the genre include Diodorus Siculus (an Augustan historian writing in Greek) and Pompeius Trogus (also Augustan, whose work was epitomized in the third century A.D. by Justin). For the three types of history see Wiseman, 'Practice and theory in Roman historiography,' (1987), 246–8 (orig. published 1981).

8. Evaluation of this picture, which has not been seriously challenged at least in so far as it refers to the style of the early historians (but see Goodyear, *CHCL* 2.269–70), is made extremely difficult by the loss of pre-Sallustian Latin historiography. For a sketch of the evolution of history from Fabius Pictor onwards see Leeman (1963), 187–90, and A. S. Gratwick in *CHCL* 2.149–52; for the techniques of the annalists see Oakley (1997), 72–99.

9. So, cautiously, Oakley (1997), 25. The standard study is B. W. Frier, *Libri Annales Pontificum Maximorum* (Rome, 1979), although almost everything concerning the *Annales* is controversial. In French see now M. Chassignet, ed., *L'Annalistique Romaine*: Tome 1, *Les Annales des Pontifes et l'Annalistique Ancienne (fragments)* (Paris, 1996),xxiii–xlii.

10. For the character of the *Annales* see Cato 77P (famines, eclipses), Cic. *Leg.* 1.6 ('nothing can be more jejune'), *De orat.* 2.52–3 (lists), Servius on Verg. *Aen.* 1.373 (names of magistrates).

11. His Greek contemporary Dionysius of Halicarnassus was even more detailed on this period; on him see E. Gabba, *Dionysius and the History of Archaic Rome* (Berkeley, 1991).

12. Bucher (1987 [1995]), an excellent discussion (quotation from p. 38).

13. For a highly illuminating discussion of the differences between such lists and narrative history see H. White, *The Content of the Form* (Baltimore/London, 1987), 1–25.

14. Purcell (1993), 141, Bucher (1987 [1995]), 20; in general P. Culham, 'Archives and alternatives in republican Rome,' *CP* 84 (1989), 100–15.

15. Cornell (1995), 4.

16. Cornell (1995), 5, 7–9.

17. Rawson (1985), 233–49.

18. See D. Fehling, *Herodotus and his 'Sources'*, trans. J. G. Howie (Leeds, 1989; orig. published 1971), a highly controversial study but one which has effectively rocked the boat.

19. Scholars often speak of a 'hard core' of factual information that was preserved, to be elaborated by freely invented details: *RICH*, 77–8, 90–3, Oakley (1997), 21.

20. Oakley (1997), 22–3. We hear of historical ballads and other kinds of oral tradition: see Cornell (1995), 10–12.

21. 'The value of the literary tradition concerning early Rome,' in K. A. Raaflaub, ed., *Social Struggles in Archaic Rome* (Berkeley, 1988), 58.

22. 'Cicero and historiography,' in *Miscellanea di Studi Classici in Onore di Eugenio Manni* (Rome, 1979) 1.318=*Studies in Greek History and Thought* (Oxford, 1988), 188, often cited as a standard discussion of the subject.

23. S. Usher, *The Historians of Greece and Rome* (London, 1969, corrected repr. Bristol, 1985); M. Grant, *The Ancient Historians* (London, 1970, repr. 1995). The quotation is from Fornara (1983), 200.

24. Review of Wiseman (1979) in *JRS* 72 (1982), 203–6.

25. See T. J. Cornell, 'The formation of the historical tradition of early Rome', in *PP*, 67–86; Wiseman (1987), esp. 293–6 (reply to Cornell's review, orig. published 1983) and 384, and *Historiography and Imagination* (Exeter, 1994).

26. *RICH*, 70–116. Cf. also T. J. Luce, 'Ancient views on the causes of bias in historical writing', *CP* 84 (1989), 16–31.

27. See e.g. C. B. R. Pelling, 'Truth and fiction in Plutarch's *Lives*', in *Antonine Literature*, ed. D. A. Russell (Oxford, 1990), 19–52 and the essays by Wiseman and Moles in C. Gill and T. P. Wiseman, edd., *Lies and Fiction in the Ancient World* (Exeter, 1993).

28. For example, Michael Crawford, in the second edition of his standard introduction to the Roman republic, acknowledges that Wiseman's 'determined assault' may result in 'a prudent agnosticism' about the early period of Rome but says that Woodman's argument is based on 'a misconception of the nature of history' – evidently taking it for granted that the nature of historical writing has not changed in the course of the last two thousand years or more (*The Roman Republic* (London, [2]1992), 220).

29. E.g. Leeman (1963), 78–81; von Albrecht (1989), 86–101. Other fragments which overlap with Livy's text are Coelius 11P (~ Livy 21.22.5) and 20P (~ Livy 22.3.11, 5.8); the story of Maharbal promising Hannibal dinner on the Capitoline (Cato 86P ~ Coelius 25P ~ Livy 22.51.1–3); and another single combat, Livy 7.26 ~ Quad. 12P (though the latter is thought not to be by Quadrigarius). For full discussion of, and commentary on, the passages in Livy's first decade see Oakley's forthcoming volumes of commentary; on literary comparisons see A. D. Vardi, *CQ* 46 (1996), 492–514.

30. For recent discussions and extensive bibliography see E. Gruen, *Culture and National Identity in Republican Rome* (London, 1993) and E. Dench, *From Barbarians to New Men: Greek, Roman, and Modern Perceptions of Peoples from the Central Apennines* (Oxford, 1995). Livy retrojects the problem of immigration into early Roman history: it is the process both by which Rome grows (beginning with the asylum: 1.8.4–6) and by which it is threatened with corrupting influences from outside (e.g. *Praef.* 11).

31. Woodman (1977), 30–45.

32. On these elements see also below, pp. 61–2; the classic study of their contribution to historiographical style is A. H. McDonald, 'The Style of Livy', *JRS* 47 (1957), 155–72.

II. SALLUST

Though history had been written at Rome since the third century B.C., the earliest historiographical works in Latin to have been preserved in their entirety are, aside from the Caesarian *commentarii*,[1] the two monographs of Gaius Sallustius Crispus (86–35 B.C.).[2] Whether or not Cicero's is a fair description of the now lost histories written before the death of Caesar (above, p. 3), some time in the 40s B.C. Sallust published two short works that were good enough to last. In the *Bellum Catilinae* (= *BC*) Sallust narrates the career of the revolutionary Catiline in the years 64–62 B.C.; the *Bellum Jugurthinum* (= *BJ*), a work of almost twice the length, explores the intertwined themes of Rome's war in north Africa against the Numidian leader Jugurtha and the concomitant political upheavals in Rome (118–105 B.C.). A third work, the *Historiae*, a five-book annalistic history of the period 78–67, was in all likelihood left unfinished at the author's death and survives only in fragments.[3]

The personality conveyed by Sallust's prefatory remarks, both in the *BC* and the *BJ*, is of a man writing history for 'delectation in disillusionment'.[4] In his *apologia* for intellectual activity he claims that history-writing is almost as good as political action; indeed, in these corrupt times, it is the only possible course for a moral Roman to take.[5] Sallust's historical works, speeches and narrative alike, bear out the truth of the dictum that 'rhetoric is the medium of thought about politics';[6] his detached approach assures that both sides of the political scene are treated with the same mistrustful, more than slightly jaundiced eye.[7] Yet his insistence in these prefaces on the utility of history, and on the possibility of learning morally sound behaviour from observing the past, makes demands on the reader beyond simply that of listening to the voice of doom. This is history that is meant to teach, even to inspire:[8] 'for I have often heard that Q. Maximus, P. Scipio, and other extremely eminent men besides were accustomed to say that when they looked at the *imagines* [portrait masks] of their ancestors, their spirit was enthusiastically fired with a desire for *uirtus*. It is evident that the wax shape itself does not have such power in it, but because of the memory of their deeds this flame grows in the breasts of outstanding men, and does not die down before their *uirtus* has equalled the reputation and glory of their ancestors.'[9]

Sallust's chief preoccupation throughout his works is with *uirtus*, that is, 'the functioning of *ingenium* [a person's inborn talent and intellectual abilities] to achieve *egregia facinora* ['outstanding deeds'], and thus to win *gloria*, by the exercise of *bonae artes*' – including energy (*industria*), hard work (*labor*), integrity (*fides*), modesty (*pudor*), and self-restraint (*continentia*).[10] His conception of *uirtus* is akin to the traditional Roman aristocratic notion – except that Sallust's is a self-made quality, that neither depends on nor is guaranteed by a person's birth, chosen activity, or class.[11] He explores this preoccupation in manifold ways: through philosophical discussion in the prefaces; through presentation of *uirtus* corrupted or perverted (as in Catiline and Jugurtha) or of *uirtus* alloyed with base elements, sometimes turning a man from the proper course altogether (as in Marius, Sulla, and Pompey); and through a comparison of two great figures, each of whom embodies an aspect of *uirtus* (Caesar and Cato). Throughout, he engages his reader's attention by emphasizing the gap between historical reality and ideal moral conduct, and by suggesting that only through understanding history, particularly the factors that have produced the present moral decline, can one learn the correct behaviour that will put Rome back on the path of *uirtus* (*BJ* 1.3). It is particularly character, observed in speech or action, that shows the dynamic quality of *uirtus*: the fact that the narratives of the monographs are clearly, and that of the *Historiae* was perhaps, focused through ambivalent figures shows Sallust's fascination with personalities that are compounded of both good and evil.[12]

Sallust's moderation does not extend to his style. Though the loss of most pre-Sallustian prose apart from Cicero makes it difficult to evaluate his contribution to his chosen genre, it is generally assumed that the way he chose to write was groundbreaking, and established a new style for the Latin historiographical language.[13] In fact, however, as F. R. D. Goodyear emphasized, Sallust had precedents in both form and content. Goodyear rightly pointed to the work of Cornelius Sisenna, whose history of the Social war and after was continued by Sallust in the *Historiae*, as a 'precedent and example' for 'adventures in expression', and to the monograph of Coelius Antipater and the early first-century autobiography of Rutilius Rufus (one of Sallust's sources for the *BJ*) as precedents for the form of the *BC* and *BJ*.[14] It is particularly relevant that some of Sisenna's favourite expressions (adverbs in *-im*, for example, and nouns in *-tudo*) are quintessentially historiographical (they will become common in Sallust, Livy, and Tacitus). Moreover, all three of Sallust's works illustrate a combination of two of the three styles that predominate in the fragments of the earlier historians: the 'purposely simple' style of Cato and Piso, and the coloured, rhetorical language – itself owing much to 'Catonian' archaism – of Coelius and Sisenna.[15] It may well be true, then, that Sallust was 'not in any obvious sense a pioneer'.[16]

Style has long been considered a reflection of the writer's character: 'le style est l'homme même' ('style is the man himself'), in Buffon's famous words. Whether or not that is true – a *persona* may well differ considerably from the writer's real self – style certainly reflects a way of seeing the world. This is especially important to bear in mind when reading history: 'the fish that the analyst of style hopes to catch is . . . nothing less than the historian's total perception of the past, the constraints within which he works and the truths he is uniquely capable of grasping . . . If we have learned anything since the Romantics – or, for that matter, since Buffon – it is that style is not the dress of thought but part of its essence.'[17] A smooth, rich, full style might mirror either a desire for political and social concord, or a concord that the author actually perceives in the events and structures forming the subject of the story. On the other hand a crabbed, difficult, elliptical style may reinforce a critical view of war or of the behaviour of political factions, and can create a linguistic atmosphere imitating the contradictions and hypocrisies in the 'real' world. Style reflects ideology.[18]

The style for which Sallust became famous was Thucydidean at heart.[19] From the Greek historian (3.82) he took the idea that because language mirrors reality, when reality is out of joint – when there is civil strife, for instance, or when politicians chase after glory, money, or power regardless of the cost – then language is misused, and the surface representation created by words has only a distorted, deceptive connection to the reality it purports to portray. As a result, people's expectations are deceived as well: the world does not work the way it appears to. Though equally capable of writing sentences full of rhetorical balance (e.g. *BJ* 1–2, 10), when it is appropriate Sallust shows the lack of coherence between words and reality by writing in a way that similarly deceives expectations. His rocky, unbalanced syntax uses connectives where they are not wanted and omits them where they are; he links non-parallel expressions by means of parallel correlatives (e.g. *BJ* 7.2 *uel ostentando uirtutem uel hostium saeuitia*, gerund ~ noun) or uses sequences that disturb the expected parallelism (a favourite is *pars . . . alii*, e.g. *BC* 2.1, *BJ* 13.8, cf. *H.* 2.8=10 and *BJ* 31.13 *pars . . . alii . . . plerique*); and he reverses the order of common expressions, especially those familiar from use in political or state language (so *militiae et domi* at *H.* 1.1 for the official *domi militiaeque*, 'at home and at war'). He defeats expectations on the level of diction as well, reaching back to the now archaic language of Cato the Elder or into the repertoire of high poetry for old-fashioned or elevated words; innovating by inventing new words or by extending Latin's syntactical range (e.g. of the future participle); or showing up the clichés of contemporary oratorical and political rhetoric by putting them in a new context in which their essential emptiness is revealed.[20]

Sallust was famous in antiquity for writing *structe*, that is, with attention to form (Fronto 2.48). Critics have found many structures in his monographs, both simple and complex, each alternative organization offering a different way of reading the history, of perceiving the relationship between the parts of the book – a richness illustrating how carefully he did write. A structure of which he was particularly fond, on both a large and a small scale, is antithesis, the opposition of contraries: at heart a rhetorical device (e.g. *militiae et domi*) it has been identified as the fundamental organizing principle of Sallust's thought. Antithesis on the level of diction or syntax enables him to make subtle connections, often forcing the reader to work hard to tease out his meaning; on the level of thought, it structures his analysis of the opposition between body and soul, energy and inertia, good and evil. More subtly, it also informs the opposition between two kinds of good, as in the comparison of Caesar and Cato in the *BC*, or two kinds of extremism, as in the balance between the speeches of Lepidus and Philippus in the *Historiae*, each of which deconstructs itself through an ironic contrast between the reader's knowledge and the speaker's hollow claims.[21]

The *Bellum Catilinae*[22]

The first, and perhaps most remarkable, feature of Sallust's first work is the preface (1–13),[23] which comprises over a sixth of the book as a whole and seems clearly to breach the convention that a preface should be proportionate to the main narrative (Lucian, *How to write history* 55).[24] Starting from the premise that men should not spend their lives in silence (*silentio*),[25] Sallust in the first two chapters of the preface argues that the mind is superior to the body and that this superiority obtains equally in war and peace (2.3 *in pace ita ut in bello*). He then uses this argument to suggest that acting well on behalf of the state (3.1 *bene facere rei publicae*) and speaking well of the state (*bene dicere*) are not essentially different activities: it is as legitimate to be distinguished in peace (*pace*: the time for writing) as in war (*bello*: the time for action), and praise is often given both to men of action and to those who have written of others' acts. But praise does not accrue in equal measure (3.2 *haudqua-quam par*) to the writer and to the practitioner, the latter here termed *auctor* in order to encourage still further the analogy between the two roles.[26] Yet, despite this inequality, the difficulty of writing about events should not be underestimated (*in primis arduom*).

Sallust offers two reasons for the difficulty of writing history. The first (*primum*) is that deeds have to be matched by words (*facta dictis exaequanda sunt*). Modern readers might assume that Sallust is here referring to a problem of *mimesis*: namely, the difficulty of representing, in the medium of narrative, events which took place over the course of time or at the same time, in the same or different places, and which involved movement, action, persons, causes, and results. This funda-mental problem, which faces every narrative historian in every age, was well recognized by Sallust's contemporary, the historian Diodorus Siculus (20.43.7), and presumably by earlier writers too.[27] But Sallust seems in fact to be referring to a rather different problem: namely, the difficulty of describing men and events in proportion to their deserts. Almost always such phrases as *facta dictis exaequare* are used in the context of finding words to describe adequately great deeds or great men (cf. *bene dicere*),[28] although occasionally the difficulty is the converse task of describing adequately some heinous crime or villain.[29]

That this is Sallust's meaning is borne out by his second reason (*dehinc*) why writing history is difficult. When the historian's task is completed, its reception by readers invariably provokes one of two reactions: if the author has criticized failings (*quae delicta reprehenderis*), he is accused of malevolence and spite; if he praises great virtue and glory (*magna uirtute atque gloria*), his words are accepted with equani-mity (*aequo animo*) only up to a certain point but disbelieved thereafter. Thus Sallust's second reason for the difficulty of writing history is complementary to the first but seen as dependent upon the readers of the completed work rather than, as in the first, upon the historian engaged in his task.[30]

At this point we might expect Sallust to claim that, by successfully negotiating the first of these difficulties, he has done his best to forestall the second. Such a claim will in effect follow later (4.3 *quam uerissume potero*, 'as truthfully as I can'), but it is preceded by a remarkable sketch of Sallust's own earlier life (3.3–4.2).[31] As a young man he was drawn by an initial enthusiasm to politics (3.3 *initio . . . studio ad rem publicam latus sum*), where many things were against him: politics was debased, and, though his *animus* rejected many symptoms of that debasement (3.4), he was at a weak stage of his life (*imbecilla aetas*), which was corrupted and gripped by ambition. Although he disagreed with the wicked behaviour of others, nevertheless the desire for honour seized him (3.5). Therefore, when he had decided to spend the remainder of his life away from politics (4.1 *mihi reliquam aetatem a re publica procul habendam decreui*), his plan was not to waste time in idle pursuits but to return to his initial enthusiasm, from which evil ambition had kept him (4.2 *a quo incepto studioque . . . eodem regressus*): he determined to write down the deeds of the Roman people in a selective manner (*carptim*),[32] as each seemed worthy of record, especially since his *animus* was now free from the hope, fear, and partisanship of political life.

Sallust's sketch of his own life falls into two parts. In the first and less creditable part (3.3–5) he defensively portrays himself at the mercy of external forces (*latus sum, aetas . . . tenebatur, me . . . uexabat*). That he was actually expelled from the senate in 50 B.C. for several years is not mentioned, though it may be alluded to in the statement that 'many things were against' him.[33] In the second and more creditable part (4.1–2) it is to Sallust himself that initiatives are attributed (*decreui, statui*). This entirely disguises the fact that his permanent departure from public life was forced upon him by charges of extortion arising from his governorship of Africa Nova in 46/45 B.C.[34] The two parts of the sketch are separated by a 'conversion', represented by Sallust's self-styled 'decision' to leave public life;[35] yet the striking feature of his new life is that he describes it as a return (*regressus*) to a pursuit which he has not previously mentioned but which is expressed in remarkably similar terms to his old life (4.2 *incepto studioque* ∼ 3.3 *initio . . . studio*). Sallust's decision consists in a vicarious return to politics through the medium of historiography,[36] a further blurring of the roles of *scriptor* and *auctor* that we encountered earlier (3.2).

Now stories of conversion are not uncommon in ancient literature,[37] and Sallust's conversion acquires moral enhancement from being modelled on Plato's Seventh Letter, where Plato describes a youth spend in discreditable society followed by a life devoted to philosophy.[38] It is in the nature of such conversions that one's new life is a moral improvement on the old; and, though Sallust does not turn to philosophy but instead returns to 'politics', we might expect him to say that on his return he has 'edited out' (cf. *carptim*) any immoral features which characterized his earlier life. Yet the opposite happens. When he announces his subject in the very next sentence, it becomes clear that it is precisely the immorality which, in the form of the Catilinarian conspiracy, he has 'edited in' (4.3–4):

igitur de Catilinae coniuratione quam uerissume potero paucis absoluam:[39] nam id facinus in primis ego memorabile existumo sceleris atque periculi nouitate.

Therefore I shall deal briefly with the conspiracy of Catiline as truthfully as I can: for I consider that action to be especially memorable for the novelty of the crime and of the danger.

His conversion turns out not to be a conversion at all but a reversion.[40]

Sallust's introduction of his subject is followed, as he explains (4.5), by a necessary character sketch of Catiline himself (5.1–8),[41] who is revealed as the child of a corrupt age (5.8). The reference to political corruption in its turn prompts Sallust to engage in a digression, in which he charts the earlier history of Rome from its beginnings to its degenerative present (5.9). This retrospective digression is lengthy (6–13) and recalls a similar digression by Thucydides (1.2.1–21.1), the historian whom above all Sallust was recognized as imitating.[42] During the course of his digression Thucydides makes the point that one cannot judge power from the physical appearance of a city: if Sparta were to be deserted, future generations would scarcely infer from its buildings that its power had been as great as its renown; conversely, if Athens were to be deserted, people would infer from its ruins that its power had been double what it really was (1.10.2). Hence one cannot infer from the smallness of Mycenae that the Trojan expedition was small; one has to rely on the evidence of Homer, who, as a poet, will have magnified its size (1.10.1, 3).

These various points recur in Sallust's digression, where they are put to a different purpose. Sallust acknowledges that Athens' achievements were quite magnificent, but 'rather less than maintained by fame' (8.2). It was because Athens produced a crop of great talents that its achievements are celebrated across the world as the greatest (8.3 *pro maxumis celebrantur*). 'So the excellence of those who acted is as great as outstanding talents were able to elevate it in words' (8.4 *extollere*).[43] Thus in this passage, which seems to constitute a digression embedded within a digression, Sallust caps the point which he had made considerably earlier in the preface (3.1–2). There he had argued for the general parity of the writer (*scriptor*) and the doer (*auctor*), while acknowledging that the latter enjoyed the greater glory. Here he makes the key point that the glory of doers depends upon writers: it seems to follow that Sallust at 8.2–4 is implicitly arguing for the primacy of writers (and hence of his own, post-conversion self) over doers.[44]

Sallust's brilliant defence of the activity of writing is symptomatic of a society which, as his own works amply demonstrate, placed a premium on military and political action.[45] The most famous parallel occurs in the elder Cato's *Origines*, an historical work which begins with a similar defence and with which Sallust was evidently extremely familiar.[46] A contemporary example is Cicero, who defends his philosophical writing on the grounds that he is compelled to endure exile (*Off*. 3.1–4). No such stigma attached to the production of literature in Greek society, and it is striking that Thucydides, despite having been exiled from Athens, nowhere attempts to defend his historiography as a substitute for politics or soldiering. There is nevertheless a parallel between Thucydides' case and that of Sallust, for, as we have seen, the latter's temporary exile from the senate in 50 B.C. was followed by a virtual but permanent exile from public life in 45 B.C.

The Augustan historian and critic, Dionysius of Halicarnassus, believed that Thucydides' exile conditioned his writing of history: he argued that Thucydides was embittered by his exile and was therefore predisposed to attack and to criticize Athens in his work.[47] Does the parallelism between Thucydides and Sallust extend as far as this? As the first sentence of Sallust's main narrative makes clear (14.1), the digression with which the preface concludes (6–13) is designed to show that Catiline represents the nadir which Rome has now reached.[48] Almost the first allegation in the main narrative is the story that Catiline, in order to marry the daughter of a former mistress, killed his own son, to whom the daughter objected (15.2), a rumour singled out by Catullus as symptomatic of contemporary frightfulness (64.401–2).[49] A later digressive passage begins with Sallust's recollection that the events of twenty years previously seemed to him by far the most wretched in the history of the Roman empire (36.4 *multo maxume miserabile*).[50] And elsewhere Roman society is described as being subjected metaphorically to earthquakes (31.1 *permota ciuitas atque inmutata urbis facies erat*, 'the community shuddered and the face of the City was transformed'), plague (36.5 *tanta uis morbi uti tabes plerosque ciuium animos inuaserat*, 'such was the virulence of the disease and (so to speak) the corruption which had invaded many of the citizens' minds'; cf. 10.6) and fire (38.1 *plebem exagitare, dein . . . magis incendere*, 'to shake the plebs, then . . .

inflame it more').[51] On the evidence of the *Bellum Catilinae* it is scarcely surprising that a historian in the second century A.D., echoing Sallust's own words at 3.2 (above, p. 14), maintained that Sallust 'criticizes his own times and attacks their failings' ('et tempora *reprehendit* sua et *delicta* carpit').[52] It certainly would not be difficult to hold that Sallust used the medium of historiography to revenge himself on the society which had twice rejected him.[53]

Yet Sallust's indictment of contemporary Rome comes oddly from one whose defence of historiography at 3.1–2 and 8.2–4 seems to rest largely on the assumption that the role of the historian is to speak well of the state or to praise it (3.1 *bene dicere*,[54] 8.3 *celebrantur*, 8.4 *extollere*). Sallust's subtle and elaborate defence of the writing of history in his preface fails to embrace the kind of historiography which he himself practises in the work as a whole.[55] This failure seems all the more stark if we consider the likely background against which Sallust's work was written.

About fifteen years before Sallust produced his *Bellum Catilinae*, Cicero had written a letter to another historian, his friend L. Lucceius, asking him to write a monograph on the Catilinarian conspiracy and its aftermath (*Fam.* 5.12). Though Cicero envisaged that Lucceius would attack Cicero's own opponents (4 *reprehendes ea quae uituperanda duces*), he saw the primary purpose of the work as being that 'my name should be illuminated and celebrated in your writing' (1 *illustretur et celebretur*). There is no evidence that Lucceius ever succumbed to Cicero's eloquent persuasion. Instead it was Sallust who took up the challenge of treating the Catilinarian conspiracy,[56] and his attitude towards Cicero is anything but straightforward heroizing.[57] The consul's First Catilinarian, which famously begins *Quo usque tandem abutere, Catilina, patientia nostra?* ('How much longer, Catiline, will you abuse our tolerance?'), is despatched with these words (31.6): 'Then M. Tullius the consul . . . delivered a sparkling speech, and useful for the state, of which he later published a written version'. What is the tone of this sentence? Is Cicero being dismissed with faint praise? Or is Sallust inhibited by the fact of the speech's publication?[58] Earlier, Sallust had put Cicero's famous exordium into the mouth of Catiline himself (20.9 *quae quo usque tandem patiemini, fortissumi uiri?*, 'How much longer will you tolerate these things, bravest of men?'): is this malicious parody or sincere compliment?[59] How significant is it that Cicero later appears as the personified protection of Rome (36.3 *Cicero urbi praesidio*)? The answers to such questions have been so varied that we may safely assume that Sallust's treatment of Cicero is far removed from that which Cicero asked of his friend Lucceius.

Even more striking is Sallust's handling of the crucial debate at which the fate of the conspirators was decided and which he prefaces with a brief introduction (50.3–5).[60] Making no reference at all to Cicero's Fourth Catilinarian, Sallust gives a very long speech to both Caesar, who speaks in favour of leniency (51.1–43), and the younger Cato, who speaks in favour of the death-penalty (52.2–36).[61] It is the latter which wins the day, and the assembled senators praise the *uirtus* of the man who was considered 'distinguished and great' (53.1 *clarus atque magnus*). This reaction is then used by Sallust to contrive a digression on the significance of *uirtus* in Roman history (53.2–5), which leads him to the statement that 'in my lifetime there have been two men of substantial *uirtus*, though of differing characteristics, M. Cato and C. Caesar' (53.6). Finally this statement in its turn is used to contrive a comparison of the two great men (54). This famous comparison, for which the technical term is a *syncrisis*, turns out to be as mystifying as Sallust's treatment of Cicero: for every reader who believes that he ranks Caesar over Cato there is another who believes exactly the opposite.[62]

No less difficult to read is the presentation of Catiline himself. Sallust makes Catiline in his first speech complain that his enemies have an abundance of riches 'which they pour into building on the sea and into levelling mountains' (20.11). This was precisely Sallust's own complaint in the introductory digression (13.1): 'by many private individuals have mountains been overturned, seas paved over'. Likewise Catiline's capacity for vigilance and toil (5.3 *patiens . . . uigiliae*, 27.2 *uigilare neque insomniis neque labore fatigari*) finds its echo in the sketch of Caesar (54.4 *Caesar . . . laborare, uigilare*). Since such parallels link Catiline either with Sallust himself or with a man of outstanding *uirtus*, it is perhaps possible to argue that the conspirator is presented as a 'mixed' or 'complex' character.[63]

On the other hand, Catiline in his introductory sketch is said to be possessed of 'an evil and twisted personality' (5.1 *ingenio malo prauo-que*), a description which seems comprehensively damning and to influence our reading of the man thereafter. If Catiline echoes an admirable sentiment of Sallust, that is no doubt an illustration of his capacity for limitless simulation (5.4 *quoius rei lubet simulator*). If he shares vigilance and toil with Caesar, we should remember the implication (5.2–3) that he displayed these qualities from adolescence in civil wars which he had welcomed and that, while in Sallust's view Caesar desired conventional arenas in which to demonstrate his *uirtus* (54.4), Catiline lusted at taking over the state (5.6 *lubido maxima . . . rei publicae capiundae*).[64] It is difficult not to agree with Syme that 'the *Bellum Catilinae* is built up around a villain'.[65]

Yet Catiline's villainy is hardly in evidence at the end of the monograph. When he finds himself cut off and with nowhere to turn, he decides to join battle with the consul C. Antonius (57.5) and, in a long passage of direct speech (58.1–21), delivers a pre-battle exhortation whose noble sentiments 'appear strangely in the mouth of a debauched conspirator against his country'.[66] Antonius for his part is ignominiously kept from the forthcoming confrontation by bad feet and is obliged to transfer command to a deputy, M. Petreius, whose own pre-battle exhortation is restricted to two lines of indirect speech (59.4–5). After the battle is joined, Catiline strikes at the enemy (60.4 *saepe hostem ferire*) as if he were a hero from the past (cf. 7.6 *quisque hostem ferire*), he performs all the activities associated with an ideal general (60.4)[67] and makes more progress than Petreius had expected (60.5). Finally, when his forces are inevitably routed by superior numbers, he is struck down while still fighting (60.7 *pugnans*), exactly as he had urged upon his troops (58.21 *pugnantes*).

It is at this moment, with the battle completed, that Sallust invites his readers directly to see (61.1 *cerneres*, 'you could see') how much boldness there had been in Catiline's army (*quanta audacia*):[68] this is the boldness in war which had characterized the early republic (9.3 *audacia in bello*), and the further echo of Catiline's speech (58.2 *quanta . . . audacia*) indicates that his confidence in the excellence of his troops had not been misplaced. Almost each man, Sallust notes, now covered with his body in death the place which he had captured by fighting while still alive (61.2: an echo of 58.10); and those few dislodged by their opponents revealed by their frontal wounds that they had died bravely (61.3).[69] Finally there was Catiline himself. Having penetrated furthest of all into the enemy ranks, he was found to be still breathing, retaining in his countenance the defiance of spirit which had distinguished him during his life (61.4 *ferociam . . . animi*). Yet, given the ways in which the reader's sympathies have been manipulated in favour of Catiline in these final pages, we seem to be far removed from the defiant spirit (*animus ferox*) which, in the introductory character sketch, was encouraged by the consciousness of his crimes (5.7 *conscientia scelerum*). Whatever interpretation we place upon Catiline earlier in the narrative, there seems no doubt that at the very end he has become 'a tragic hero'.[70]

The second-century A.D. historian Florus, after quoting Sallust's description of Catiline's body (61.4), adds: 'the finest of deaths – if he had fallen thus for his country' (2.12.12).

The *Bellum Jugurthinum*

Structure and themes

Causation is one of Sallust's preoccupations. In each of his works he identifies a plurality of starting points: the beginning of social decline at Rome; the beginning of deep political and social corruption; the point at which the crisis that is his particular topic began.[71] One consistent turning-point is the destruction of Carthage and the consequent removal of the so-called *metus Punicus* ('fear of Carthage') or *metus hostilis* ('fear of the enemy') in 146 B.C.: that is, the theory that as long as the Romans faced a strong external threat, they would remain united in self-defence and their civil affairs would remain peaceful as a result.[72] According to Sallust's analysis, the Jugurthine war stemmed from the cataclysmic combination of the Numidian prince Jugurtha and the Roman nobles who dominated the corrupt society that was spinning out of control in the mid-second century. But the war was itself the origin of still greater conflict. Sallust had used the story of Catiline to illustrate the internal problems of the state at a particular point in time; in the *BJ* he expands those parameters, analysing the interplay between foreign and domestic upheavals and tracing their implications for the future (his past).[73] The *BJ* stands halfway between a monograph and annals: the person of Jugurtha provides a formal focus and unity to the narrative akin to that provided by the subject of a biography, but the narrative reaches beyond its own boundaries in a way that the *BC* does not.[74] Its extended narrative spans more than a dozen years with a rough chronological organization by consul (cf. 43.1, 109 B.C.; 73.7, elections for 107)[75] and the alternation of *res externae* ('foreign affairs') and *res internae* ('domestic affairs') characteristic of annals,[76] while Sallust's treatment of the political issues, in particular, gives the sense that the story being told is only part of a larger whole. Though the Numidian war eventually ends, we are not given the narrative satisfaction of seeing Jugurtha die; moreover, Sallust repeatedly reminds us that the Roman characters will play crucial roles in the battles of the late republic, which in turn prepare for the Caesarian civil war.[77] Historically, Jugurtha's ambition and guerilla tactics were largely an irritation and embarrassment to Rome;[78] for Sallust, the story provides a convenient means by which to investigate Marius' rise to power and the origins of his conflict with Sulla, which would eventually lead to the devastation of Italy and of its republican government.

Yet if Sallust's 'real' interest in this second monograph is the Roman political system, his treatment of the *res externae* is not perfunctory: the topography and people of Numidia, together with their leader Jugurtha, are topics of intellectual and thematic importance.[79] The length and scope of the story mirror the expanse of the country in which much of the action takes place; the tactics necessary for fighting a guerilla war, with its constantly changing stratagems and deceptive appearances, find their analogue in the nomadic character of the Numidians, whose volatility makes them eager for revolution (46.3, 66.2). At the start of the war narrative proper, Sallust establishes the connection between geography, ethnography, and theme in a formal description of the province (17–19); he returns to the land repeatedly, above all to its lack of defining features (and hence to the almost magical quickness with which those who are familiar with the terrain can move about in it: 75.1, 92.5) and to its disorienting sands (53.1, 79.6). Jugurtha himself is the focus of this thematics of disorder, interposing delay, deception, and an almost hallucinatory mobility between himself and the Romans, keeping them from taking control.[80]

The first third of the monograph focuses closely on Jugurtha's career, moving from his youth (6) through his military training (7–8) and the death of his adoptive father Micipsa (11), followed by his ascension to sole power after murdering his step-brothers (12–21) and by the first stages of war, which culminate in his victory over the Roman army under the command of Aulus Albinus (38–9).[81] Each contact between Jugurtha and the Romans results in some kind of illicit delay, exchange, or disorder, in both the military and the domestic arenas: Roman legates are kept from meeting those they are sent to contact (22.5); a surrender is arranged in which Jugurtha promises one thing openly but negotiates a second, secret bargain (29.5); Roman armies are deluded, engagements deferred or complicated by mirage and masquerade); above all, constant bribery and unregulated exchange of goods corrupt the Romans and defer settlement of any kind.[82]

This persistent refusal of closure extends to the monograph's political theme, which is structured around the contrived but traditional antithesis of the plebs versus the nobles, who are labelled at the outset as 'proud' (5.1 *superbiae*).[83] This, too, is affected by Jugurtha's affinities with chaos. The long-standing antagonism between the orders is worsened by the Roman aristocratic commanders' connivance with Jugurtha and their consequent surrender in the field, until eventually the balance of power in Rome is tipped far enough for the plebeian leadership to take direct action against the senate, first through radical rhetoric (31), then by means of legislation (40). Sallust marks the kinship between the military and political realms by punctuating this first third of the monograph by two digressions, the African excursus (17–19, see above) and the chapters on the 'nature of the political parties and factions' in which he analyses the pernicious and widespread power of Roman political factions (41–2), balanced ethnographies bracketing the complex interaction between Jugurtha and Rome.

The second main section (43–83) belongs to Q. Caecilius Metellus Numidicus, the first commander to have a measure of success against Jugurtha. He brings with him, however, the twin seeds of his own destruction: his opposition to the plebs, later specified as *superbia* ('pride'), a rare fault in a character that is otherwise laudably fair (43.1, 45.1); and his lieutenant, one Gaius Marius (46.7). The pride is formally introduced, though it does not manifest itself until later (64.1); the lieutenant, on the other hand, slips into the narrative, his official presentation delayed until he reveals his true ambition, the consulate, at which point Sallust gives him a formal character sketch (63–4). Metellus' progress against Jugurtha is considerable, and, though he cannot bring the war to a close, he manages to reduce the prince to despair, increasing his normal tendency to disorder and rapid mobility (72.2, 76.1), while also restoring order to the armies that had been corrupted and dispersed by their contact with Jugurthine tactics (44–5). Part of Metellus' success stems from his use of sieges as opposed to the open battles that had ruined Albinus (38) and nearly destroyed his own troops (50–3): attacks on towns, which owe less to chance and stratagems of deceit, are much more to the Romans' taste than Jugurtha's slippery guerilla warfare. Concomitantly, Metellus shows an ever-increasing ability to turn Jugurtha's own stratagems against him, a case of using like to beat like.

But it is Marius who is most like Jugurtha, and who consequently will be most effective against him in this mythico-historical narrative in which it takes a beast to kill a beast. The monograph's final section opens with his election to the consulate – an election which, as he is a self-made *nouus homo* ('new man'), overturns traditional categories and expectations.[84] Jugurthine disorder here enters Roman political life with a vengeance. Though Marius' particular brand of chaos is political, his first consular act is a blend of the political and the military: he enrolls an army not, as was usual, from the wealthy classes (*non more maiorum neque ex classibus*) but according to individuals' desire (*lubido*), as Sallust puts it: that is, he takes volunteers, most of whom are eager for the spoils of war (84.3–4, 86.2).[85] The unregulated exercise of *lubido* is one of Sallust's favourite symptoms of chaos, evoking the transgression of boundaries that inevitably accompanies revolution. The new Marian army challenges the basis on which Roman armies had traditionally been recruited (only those with property, i.e. with a vested financial interest in the state, were previously eligible to serve); while Sallust does not dwell on the change *per se*, simply describing it in a couple of sentences, he highlights it by giving Marius a lengthy speech of exhortation (85) explicitly designed to encourage enlistment and to irritate the nobility (84.5). This substantial narrative pause – it is the longest speech in the monograph – is Marius' opportunity to elaborate his personal and political credo, and as such it functions as an elaborate demonstration of his own boundary-crossing *lubido*, his double desire for personal advancement and political change.

Direct speech is carefully apportioned in the *BJ*, as in the *BC* (below, p. 44 n. 61). Of the three full-scale formal orations, all are delivered by relative outsiders: the Numidian prince Adherbal (14: four OCT pages), the radical tribune Memmius (31: three and a half OCT pages), and the plebeian consul Marius (85: five and a half OCT pages). Only briefly do we hear the voice of the traditional Roman aristocrat – a short letter from Scipio (9.2), a senatorial communication (104.5), 'a few words' from the eloquent Sulla (102.5–11). The situation is even worse than in the *BC*, where balancing Catiline's two dangerous, seductive orations (*BC* 20, 58) we at least heard from two exemplars (however partial) of old-fashioned *uirtus*, Caesar and Cato. Now, in all his works, Sallust took Thucydides' famous description of the stasis at Corcyra (3.82) very much to heart, repeatedly evoking that atmosphere of civil disorder in which the slipperiness of words at once reflects and creates a moral and political chaos that is ultimately as labile and invasive as any disease (cf. esp. *BJ* 41.9 *inuadere*: above, p. 17). It is axiomatic in much ancient political thought that the truly 'good' should speak a steady, truthful language in which words correspond to reality, while those who seek change and who favour the non-aristocratic classes speak cleverly but dangerously, able – in Aristophanes' famous words (*Clouds* 882–4) – to make the weaker argument the stronger. The fact that the aristocratic voice is relatively mute in the *BJ* might suggest that demagogic rhetoric has simply taken its place; but in fact Sallust is more subtle than that. His speakers are far from upholding traditional ideals, but what they offer in their place is a challenge rather than a defeat. So we hear from a foreign ally whose values are more Roman than those of the corrupt Romans; an incendiary plebeian demagogue who makes a fair amount of sense; and a charismatic military leader who himself inverts the conventional aristocratic charges against sophistic speech: clever rhetorical training is an élite preserve, Marius says, with which the senators have masked their incompetence, used fancy words as a substitute for their non-existent deeds, deceived, cajoled, and oppressed the poor.

Marius' radical speech eloquently presents the new *uirtus* of the *nouus homo*. In the narrative of the *BJ*, it aligns him with the foreigner Adherbal and the tribune Memmius, both of whom speak on behalf of groups at the mercy of the aristocratic government. It has critical differences from those speeches, however. Though delivered in order to irritate the aristocracy (84.5 *nobilitatem exagitandi causa*), it *is* a speech by a consul and as such marks Marius' entrance into the aristocratic government that he professes to despise. As Sallust has already remarked, at this time plebs and nobles behave similarly (40.5). The political turmoil caused by Marius' election is not a final one, to be followed by a new domestic peace under a new dispensation; rather, it heralds more of the same.

When Marius arrives in Africa with his revolutionary army (86.4), his military successes drive Jugurtha to increasingly desperate measures, until the prince practically fades out of the picture: he last participates actively in the narrative at 101, where he escapes the carnage of his army's defeat. But as Metellus was shadowed from the beginning by his own replacement, so Marius soon faces a rival, the man who will be largely responsible for ending the war: L. Cornelius Sulla arrives during the siege of Jugurtha's fort on the Muluccha. His appearance comes close on the heels of a hard-won victory in which Marius barely avoids yet another stalemate (94.7 'thus Marius' rashness, corrected by chance, snatched glory from blame'). Sulla's presence demands attention: his entrance mandates both a formal character sketch (95) and a brief discussion of his model relationship with soldiers and consul alike (96). This formal introduction effectively contrasts with Sallust's treatment of Marius, whom he mentions ten times before officially introducing him at 63.2–7. These different entrances into the narrative reflect traditional views in Roman literature of the men's respective social positions. Marius the *nouus*, eager for revolution (*nouae res*), infiltrates the military narrative as part of the *nobilis* Metellus' cohort, gradually becoming visible owing to his own exceptional talent and because he attracts the notice of the divine, a soothsayer at Utica who predicts his future greatness (63.1). The mythico-historical paradigm for his story is that of Servius Tullius, the slave's child who came to the notice of King Tarquinius Priscus after a divine omen; he eventually became king, instituted great reforms, and, if he had not been assassinated, would perhaps have ended the monarchy altogether (Livy 1.39–48).[86] Sulla, on the other hand, as befits a patrician, arrives with some panoply, interrupting the narrative. But like contemporary Roman society, in which corruption has pervaded both the orders, Sulla's aristocratic gloss cannot hide the fact that his acts and character are destined not only to bring ruin to the state but also to compromise the honesty or offend the propriety of the historians who try to write his *res gestae*.[87]

It is in fact Sulla who, in a series of involved negotiations, engineers the betrayal of Jugurtha and hands him over to Marius (113.7). The moment itself receives only brief attention, before Sallust steps back to report with curious obliqueness the final acts of the war: 'At the same time a battle against the Gauls was lost by our generals Q. Caepio and Cn. Mallius, which shook all Italy with fear. For the Romans then considered – and indeed have done so right up to our own time – that while all other things are easy targets for our valour, we fight with the Gauls for our lives, not just for glory. But after it was reported that the war in Numidia was finished and Jugurtha was being brought in chains to Rome, Marius was elected consul *in absentia* and the province of Gaul was assigned to him. As consul he triumphed on the first of January with great glory. And at that time the hopes and resources of the state were all placed in him.'[88] A return to Rome at the end of a campaign is characteristic of military narratives; in the *BJ* it closes both the final section and the book as a whole by forming a bracket with Marius' first election and recruiting activities (84–6), and with the announcement of Sallust's theme (5.1–2).[89] We return as well in this final paragraph to the structuring device of the hero's life span: the combination of Jugurtha's transport to Rome and Marius' triumph would imply to all Roman readers that he would be executed as Marius reached the height of his *gloria*.[90] It is ultimately not any closing event, however, but instead Marius' beginning that this ending celebrates. He triumphs on the first day of the new year after being reelected consul; the iterated title in the penultimate sentence underscores his exceptional reappointment (he would hold four more consulships in the next five years). The first of those consulships fades in importance, becoming a foil to the second, as the great glory accruing to his victory over Jugurtha sets the stage for the far more serious fight impending against the Gauls. This last paragraph, in closing the Jugurthine war and opening up another campaign, contributes to the sense that the *BJ* is part of a larger whole, annalistic history in embryo – and given what we know about Marius' future and his war with Sulla, the hopes of the people with which Sallust ends must give us a terrible foreboding.[91]

Jugurtha and Carthage

Jugurtha's affinity with and ability to produce a chaos that profoundly affects Roman military and political stability have been sketched above; but he possesses exceptionally good qualities as well. He has *uirtus*, intelligence, and great military skill; he is loved rather than envied by his peers (6.1), a remarkable achievement in the atmosphere of envy (*inuidia*) that conventionally attends excellence; and his talents eventually lead Scipio Aemilianus to regard Jugurtha as his right-hand man, while other Romans hasten to patronize him (7–8). All of these are Roman qualities: the only specifically Numidian activity he is said to pursue is hunting (6.1) – incidentally a training for war among Roman youth as well. In this mixture of corruption and *uirtus* Jugurtha resembles Marius, Sulla, Catiline, and Caesar: great figures who combine, in Syme's words, 'energy and criminal ambition'.[92] In particular, Jugurtha is in some senses a double for Marius. They served together under Scipio at Numantia and probably knew one another, a well-known fact which Sallust does not mention but which he invites us to recall by dwelling on Jugurtha's close relations with the Romans in Scipio's entourage (7.6 '(Scipio) considered him among his friends . . .', 7.7 '(Jugurtha) had bound many to him with friendship'); they each come from nowhere to displace a 'rightful' (i.e. high-born) leader; finally, Jugurtha essentially vanishes from the narrative as Marius becomes the dominant character.[93] In the narrative economy of the monograph, Jugurtha and Marius are in some senses interchangeable – fittingly enough, as the latter will go on to do the damage to Rome that Jugurtha wanted to, but could not.

Unlike Marius, however, Jugurtha is also an African. In the Roman imagination of the late republic, that heritage aligns him with the other great African enemies, Cleopatra, with whom he is linked by Propertius in a poem celebrating Augustus' triumph after Actium (4.6.65–6), and the Carthaginian Hannibal, who similarly blended great virtue and great faults (cf. Livy 21.4) Hannibal plays no part in the *BJ*, but his city – even though at the time of the Jugurthine war it no longer existed – has an important place both in the narrative and in Sallust's historical imagination. Indeed, a pronounced effect of identifying this relatively insignificant African war as a primary cause of the devastation of Italy (5.1–2) is to draw attention to Carthage and to the effects of its removal.

Like Jugurtha, Carthage is paradoxical, composite. As the city whose external threat kept Rome from collapsing into internal disorder, whose enmity made Roman political concord possible, and whose destruction in 146, at the height of Roman military success in the Mediterranean, Sallust identifies as the first cause of Rome's decline, Carthage naturally acquires an almost magical aura. It appears three times in the *BJ*, in each of the three authorial digressions (the Carthaginians themselves are mentioned more often, e.g. 5.4, 14.10, 81.1; but they do not participate significantly in the war). Each time it is mentioned, the city stabilizes actual or potential disorder: paradox within paradox, as its own composite nature – the virtuous enemy, the danger that makes safe – ought to keep it from producing unity.[94]

The city of Carthage enters the *BJ* at the culmination of the African ethnography: 'later the Phoenicians . . . founded Hippo, Hadrumetum, Lepcis, and other cities along the shore . . . about Carthage, I think it is better to be silent than to say too little, since time admonishes me to hasten to another topic.'[95] Sallust's silence in the face of a topic that is too much to handle is conventional (cf. e.g. Strabo 9.1.16 on Athens); here the convention conveys the city's power and fascination. Better to say nothing than to say too little: the bulk and importance of Carthage threaten to take over the historian's project, to divert him from his task. Turning instead to geography, he then briefly sketches the different African territories, paying special attention to the Carthaginian boundaries and the shifting sands of the Syrtes, both of which will become important later (see below): 'and so toward Catabathmos, the place which separates Egypt from Africa, as you go along the coast Cyrene comes first . . . and then the two Syrtes and Lepcis between them, then the Altars of the Philaeni, a place which the Carthaginians considered the border of their empire in the direction of Egypt, and afterwards other Punic cities.'[96] The borders of Carthage appear again in the final short paragraph detailing the rulers of the African provinces at the time of the war (19.7). In its first appearances, then, Carthage is both unspeakable and a place that delimits, marking the borders of Sallust's own current historiographical project and of a narrative section therein.

In the second of the monograph's digressions, the Roman political ethnography (41–2), Carthage appears in the familiar guise of the *metus hostilis*, put in counterpoise to discord and wandering on a metaphorical level. This digression is Sallust's response to the Mamilian commission, the plebeian attempt to identify and curb patrician corruption (40): in it, he anatomizes social and political corruption in Rome after the third Punic war and the Gracchan reforms of the following decades. Carthage, the weight which kept Roman power from turning on itself and spinning out of control, leads off his analysis, forming as in the African excursus a boundary marker (41.2, 3 'for before Carthage was destroyed'; 'but when that fear had left men's minds'). What Carthage controls here is the maintenance of categories: without it trustworthy distinctions and definitions break down, bad things arise from good, success generates disaster, *libertas* ('freedom') becomes *lubido* ('desire,' 41.3, 5). Power and greed, qualities that respect no limits, invade the state, considering nothing worthwhile or out-of-bounds: the effect, says Sallust, was like an earthquake.[97]

Finally, towards the end of Metellus' command in Africa, messengers come to ask the Romans to settle an incipient civil war in Lepcis Magna, a city formerly in Punic territory. Though Metellus sends four cohorts (77.4), what happens to them is not narrated; the narrative impulse turns instead to an excursus on an ancient boundary dispute between Carthage and Cyrene, the next great city to the east (78–9). Lepcis played no part in this dispute, other than to be situated in the middle of the desert whose shifting sands, like the Syrtes (the coastal sand banks), prevent the rival powers from fixing their borders.[98] The heart of the digression is the story of the 'outstanding and wondrous deed' (79.1) of two Carthaginians, the Philaeni brothers, who, in an effort to settle the dispute between their city and Cyrene, agree to be buried alive in the desert (79.8–9). Henceforth, their tomb and the altar there erected mark the line between the territories. For the third time in the narrative, then, Carthage fixes a stable point, here defining the boundary between two discordant groups. This final digression is carefully linked to the other two: the civil discord of Lepcis (77.1) recalls the excursus on party politics, while we have already met the Altars of the Philaeni at the end of the section on Punic territory in the African ethnography (19.3).

These two composite elements, Jugurtha and Carthage, thus have opposite effects, the one producing disorder and challenging limits, the other marking stability and constituting a boundary (*fines*) both in the text and in history.[99] The city's destruction finally removes the greatest threat to Roman security; paradoxically, however, it also unleashes the forces of disorder and corruption, both within Rome and without, in the person of Jugurtha.

The *Historiae*

'In these diverse ways, the lost masterpiece becomes palpable – content, architecture, and tone.' – '[I]n my judgement the most learned and acute scholars have often been over-confident in delineating the scope of lost histories and the qualities of their authors.' [100]

So two eminent ancient historians on the problems of interpreting a fragmentary text such as the *Historiae*. Sallust's last work has come down to us in various ways: four speeches and two letters were excerpted, probably in the imperial period, and have their own manuscript tradition; there are a very few manuscript and papyrus fragments of other parts of the work (e.g. *H.* 3.94=64 and 98=66 on the campaigns of 73 B.C.); and many short quotations, allusions, and paraphrases are found in the texts of grammarians and other ancient scholars. Finally, the *Historiae* was used by later writers, e.g. the elder Pliny in his *Natural History* and Plutarch in his *Life* of Sertorius, from which some details of Sallust's work can be inferred.[101] Enough, in terms of sheer quantity, has survived to give us some idea – if not a palpable sense – of its scope and some of its qualities. Following an annalistic format, the narrative alternated between *res internae* and *externae* (above, p. 21);[102] there were at least three formal geographical excursuses; and the story itself was focussed on its major characters, a concentration on the deeds of great men befitting this type of history, i.e. *res gestae*.

Any relatively cautious treatment of the *Historiae* will tend toward the atomizing, as the individual pieces lend themselves to a commentary format rather than a synthetic approach. Our view of the whole has naturally been skewed by the accidents of transmission – the speeches and letters, in particular, have received attention disproportionate to the amount they would perhaps have received had they been preserved in their original narrative context (indeed, until Reynolds' 1991 OCT they were the only fragments regularly included in editions of Sallust's other works). In general, the *Historiae* makes exceptional demands on the reader, who is forced not only to try to interpret the text but first (and concomitantly, since no reconstruction of fragments is ever final) to reconstruct, fill in the gaps, try to see the original picture. Still, one can suggest possible directions for thinking about this annalistic history, and in particular about the three elements which stand out in the fragments: Sallust's prefatory comments on his profession, his character assessments, including the long portions of *oratio recta*, and the ethnogeographical descriptions.

In his preface, Sallust clearly chose a different route from the philosophical approach of the monographs. He does not seem to have returned to the mind-body antithesis of the *BC*, or to the lament on contemporary decline of the *BJ*; instead, an evaluation of other historians preceded an overview of the years leading up to his chosen period.[103] Several fragments show that Sallust deployed the major conventions of historiographical introductions, beginning with the opening words:[104] *Res populi Romani M. Lepido Q. Catulo consulibus ac deinde militiae et domi gestas conposui* (1.1 'I have composed the military and political history of the Roman people from the consulate of Marcus Lepidus and Quintus Catulus onward'). Sallust here identifies his genre as *annales*, history organized by the series of annual magistrates (*consulibus*), and his particular starting-point as 78 B.C. (the year of the two eponymous consuls).[105] Such history is theoretically without fixed stopping-point (*ac deinde*): as Rome continues forever, so may the record of its achievements.[106] The sentence also indicates Sallust's general subject matter, Roman history (*Res p. R. . . . gestas*) and its specific content, military and political (*militiae et domi*). The juxtaposed *populus Romanus* and consuls, together enclosed by the hyperbaton (dislocated word order) of *Res . . . gestas*, iconically inscribes two essential components of Roman history, people and leaders, within the dynamic purpose of the state.[107] The last word, *conposui* ('I have arranged/composed'), describes the writer's activity as one of organization and artistic structure, appropriately capping the verbal architecture of the rest of the sentence. Finally, one late-antique scholar who cites the line uses it to illustrate metrical shapes in prose: *Res populi Romani* is the first hemistich of a hexameter, and Sallust our earliest extant example of a Latin historian beginning his narrative with a nod toward historical epic,[108] a genre acknowledged repeatedly since Herodotus as the precursor of historiography.[109]

Sallust went on to discuss his predecessors, including Cato (1.4=3) and – probably – Sisenna (1.2=4). He commented both on their quality

(Cato was 'the most eloquent of the Roman race,' while a now unnamed writer – sometimes also thought to be Cato – distorted the truth: 1.5=Unc. Ref. 2) and on his own place among them (1.3=5 'I in such a great crowd of very learned men'). Comparing his own work with that of his predecessors has two primary effects. First, it situates Sallust in the 'profession' (he is, by implication, himself a 'learned man') in much the same way as the first sentence establishes the *bona fides* of the book itself; second, it allows him to challenge, either explicitly or implicitly, the achievement of the historians who precede him. We do not know how he compared or contrasted his own status with the throng, but when Livy quotes this part of the proem (*Praef.* 3) he does so to suggest, with characteristic disingenuousness, that he himself will stand out despite the numbers of other writers; Tacitus – also characteristically – comes right out and says that previous imperial historiography is bunk (e.g. *H.* 1.1.1–2, *A.* 1.1.2).[110] Finally, Sallust claims that he is free from bias: *neque me diuorsa pars in ciuilibus armis mouit a uero* ('nor has the fact that I fought on a different side in the civil wars moved me from the truth,' 1.6=7), a conventional claim echoed by Livy, *Praef.* 5: *omnis expers curae quae scribentis animum, etsi non flectere a uero, sollicitum tamen efficere posset* ('free from every concern which, though it cannot move a writer's mind from the truth, can nevertheless worry it'). The same theme will recur in Tacitus' famous remarks at *H.* 1.1.3 'Galba, Otho, and Vitellius were known to me neither on account of any favour nor any injury' and *A.* 1.1.3 'thence it is my plan to relate a few last things concerning Augustus . . . without anger or favouritism, reasons for which I keep at a distance.'[111] In Sallust's words the detail *diuorsa pars* may have been part of a discussion, parallels to which are found in the *BC* and *BJ*, of his own previous political involvement.

Personalities

In his famous discussion of the 'rules' of *historia*, Cicero emphasizes the importance of character in any telling or interpretation of the past: 'you need . . . to reveal not only what was said or done but also in what manner, and . . . . to explain all the reasons, whether they be of chance or intelligence or impetuousness, and also to give not only the achievements of any famous protagonist but also his life and character' *(De orat.* 2.63; similar are Sempronius Asellio 1P, Livy *Praef.* 9). Ancient history was not history of the *longue durée* but of individual actors, usually

members of the ruling élite or their antagonists, whose deeds formed a
linked chain of achievements that sustained and propelled the state
forward.[112] Indeed, as time progressed, military and political history
moved closer to biography, as power in those areas was increasingly
concentrated in the hands of a few, and eventually of a single man. Both
the monographs and the fragments of the *Historiae* indicate that Sallust
shared this interest in character as a moral and a political phenomenon,
which above all provides a means of explaining historical events.
(Following the ancients' lead, one dominant school of modern Roman
history is dedicated to prosopography, the study of political and military
careers.)

Two primary modes of characterization in literature have been
identified, the direct (via explicit comments by the author, formal
character sketches, etc.) and the indirect (showing character through a
person's words or actions, by analogy with their personal habits, etc.).[113]
One of the primary vehicles for character assessment in ancient history
was the obituary, in which the historian himself evaluates the life and
deeds of the dead; according to the elder Seneca (*Suas.* 6.21), Sallust
introduced this device to Latin historiography.[114] No formal obituary
notices from the *Historiae* survive, but the anecdote illustrating the
character of Q. Caecilius Metellus Pius uses some of the same techniques (2.70=59):

But Metellus, having returned . . . to Farther Spain, was beheld with a great feeling of
glory on the part of those who came running from all sides. . . . [They] entertained him
in a manner far beyond normal Roman or indeed normal human practice. The house
was decked with tapestries and decorations, and stages were created for actors' display;
at the same time the ground was sprinkled with saffron and [there were] other features in
the style of a magnificent temple. In addition to that, when he was seated a statue of
Victory let down by a rope and accompanied by artificial thunder placed a crown on his
head; then as he advanced he was worshipped with incense as if he were a god. He
generally wore the *toga picta* when reclining at table. The courses were very recherché,
including not only products of the entire province but many kinds of birds and animals
previously unknown from Mauretania across the seas. With this kind of behaviour
Metellus considerably diminished his glory, especially in the estimation of serious and
old-fashioned men, who judged these things arrogant, insupportable, and unworthy of
Roman *imperium*.[115]

This extraordinary description of the general's celebration, in which
consumption of rare delicacies 'previously unknown' metonymically
represents his consumption of power (and, by extension, Roman
conquest),[116] is followed not by Sallust's own evaluation of the scene
but by his report of the 'serious and old-fashioned men' who condemn

Metellus' behaviour. Despite this distancing, however, this is a judgment
to which Sallust has carefully led the reader, both directly (by the
historian's own comment, e.g. 'in a manner far beyond normal Roman
or indeed normal human practice') and indirectly, by the particular
items he chooses to describe and by his repeated use of words inviting us
to consider the nature of Metellus' self-representation (i.e. 'a manner,'
'in the style of,' 'as if,' all of which ask us to think about comparison and
standards). Reinforcing these – and indeed dominating the anecdote –
are the expressions for seeing. The whole scene is cast as a spectacle
both for the internal audiences, who run to see Metellus and who
evaluate his acts, and for the reader, who is invited to share in the
viewing by the accumulation of visual details. The spectacular qualities
of the anecdote are complex: the house in which Metellus is entertained
with such damning luxury is fitted out for a theatrical performance in
which Metellus himself plays the part of a god. The Romans both
courted and feared this type of display, seeing elaborate histrionic
spectacle as a locus of deceit and pretence that could elevate a human
beyond his station: which is indeed what happens here.[117] The scene
may, finally, be read as a parody of a triumphal celebration, the ultimate
Roman display, in which the old men – who also play the part of the
historian, evaluating Metellus' conduct – take over the role of the slave
who was meant to remind the *triumphator* of his mortality.[118]

Equally typical of the direct method is the epigram, memorable and
incisive, distilling the essentials of a character. Here style became a
particularly important vehicle for conveying meaning, as can be clearly
seen in Tacitus, whose paradoxical language reinforces a view of the
world in general and of Roman leaders in particular as unexpected, even
monstrous.[119] The technique is not original with Tacitus: he draws on a
tradition refined by Sallust, Livy, and Velleius. In the case of the
Historiae, the fact that these *bons mots* have been removed from their
original context exaggerates their apophthegmatic nature; bearing that
in mind, however, we can still see in them important elements of the
historian's narrative technique.[120]

Two particularly characteristic epigrammatic forms are found in the
fragments. First, the use of what has been called the 'loaded alternative,'
a syntactical structure in which the historian offers two or more
explanations for an action, refusing to choose between them, but often
indicating via emphasis, word order, etc. which he appears to think most
probable. The responsibility for evaluating the truth devolves on the
reader; the writer, on the other hand, having presented more than one

possible alternative, preserves an air of evenhandedness and intellectual rigour.[121] In its effect the technique is not unlike the oratorical device of *praeteritio* ('passing by') or *occultatio* ('hiding'), which ancient rhetorical handbooks recognized as particularly damaging, as for instance at *Rhetorica ad Herennium* 4.37: 'This figure is useful if employed in a matter which it is not pertinent to call specifically to the attention of others, because there is advantage in making only an indirect reference to it, or because the direct reference would be tedious or undignified or cannot be made clear or can easily be refuted.'

Though Tacitus refined the loaded alternative, its use far antedates him. Caesar (*BC* 2.27.2 *siue uere quam habuerant opinionem ... perferunt siue etiam auribus Vari seruiunt*) shows a characteristic choice between a flattering and a pejorative reason (were Caesar's men telling the truth or were they telling Varus what he wanted to hear?), while Claudius Quadrigarius (89P *quod utrum neglegentia partim magistratum an auaritia an calamitate populi Romani euenisse dicam nescio*) offers alternatives comprising human reasons (negligence or avarice) and a supernatural one (fate bringing disaster on the Roman people).[122] In the *Historiae*, Sallust tells us that the notorious Verres 'was under suspicion of having formed an alliance for booty with the bandits, though it was uncertain whether he had truly done so or whether [he only seemed to have] through carelessness' (4.53=54 *suspectus ... fuit, incertum uero an per neglegentiam, societatem praedarum cum latronibus composuisse*). Neither alternative is flattering, though negligence is less culpable than treason; but either way, Verres is damned not by Sallust but by report (one can compare the use of the *ueteres* in judging Metellus Pius, above).

A second and related form of epigram is the one-liner. This may take many syntactical shapes, though comparative expressions and *nisi*–clauses dominate; its sting depends on its use of the unexpected and often – like the loaded alternative – on its offering an invidious choice.[123] One finds the coyly nasty remark, for instance on Cn. Cornelius Lentulus Clodianus: *perincertum stolidior an uanior* (4.1 'it was entirely uncertain whether he was more churlish or more unreliable'); the invitation to draw an unflattering distinction between near-synonyms, as on M. Lollius Palicanus: *loquax magis quam facundus* (4.43=38 'verbose rather than eloquent'); and – most characteristically – the apparent compliment suddenly withdrawn: *modestus ad alia omnia, nisi ad dominationem* (2.17=18 '[Pompey was] moderate in all things except in his thirst for power').[124]

The second major type of characterization, the indirect, needs a larger context than either epigram or anecdote, and is therefore harder to identify in a fragmentary text. Outside the speeches, however (see below), there are some hints of how Sallust may have worked. Sertorius, a popular hero, proudly bore his war wounds as proof of the valour that won him glory (1.88=77); this is a kind of characterization by analogy, in which a person's clothes, surroundings, etc. provide clues to their character.[125] Moreover, a man whom Sallust apparently admired, Sertorius, sought 'a reputation for justice and virtue in the midst of civil war' (1.90=79) – a remark which, when set in the larger context provided by Plutarch's *Life*, seems to be intended positively, but which points nonetheless with epigrammatic *paraprosdokian* ('surprise') to an inherent contradiction in the way the world was working at the time, and hence in the way we have to read the characters of the actors in that world. Finally, the man whom some have seen as the hero – and some the anti-hero – of the *Historiae*, Pompey the Great, showed skill and strength as a youth ((2.23=19 'he competed in jumping with the agile, in running with the swift, in the crowbar with the strong'), skills that not infrequently accompany the kind of popular, charismatic leader's character that we see also in Hannibal, Catiline, or Jugurtha (e.g. Sall. *BJ* 6.1 'he would ride and throw the javelin and compete in running with his peers'[126]). If Sallust did not go on to comment explicitly on Pompey's character, his use of the convention on its own could have suggested a latent danger in the young man. Similarly, Pompey's youthful belief that he could rival Alexander the Great spoke volumes (3.88=84).

But the plainest way of characterizing people is through the words that a writer puts in their mouths – and here the fragments are, if anything, disproportionately rich. Speeches in historiography served a multiplicity of narrative and thematic needs, from introducing variety to creating dramatic effect (in the literal sense, by bringing historical actors to 'life') to offering a historian different voices with which to explore complex political and social issues. The speeches in Thucydides and Cassius Dio, on the Greek side, and in Sallust, on the Latin, are perhaps the most famous instances of the use of composed orations as a means of extended political analysis.[127] Moreover, these speeches can and often do explore issues of contemporary as well as historical relevance: so the orations of Lepidus and Philippus, for example, from Book 1, examine from either side of the coin the relative merits of popular and oligarchical government, the status and sincerity of political slogans, and the dangerous question of civil war – all fresh, painful questions to Sallust's readers.

Not only do the orations and letters function as a kind of editorial page, but their rhetorical *personae* deepen our picture of each speaker, both as a type and as an individual.[128] For example, Licinius Macer, the plebeian tribune and annalist, speaks like a *popularis* historian, citing many past precedents of the plebs' successful opposition to the patriciate and of the senate's oppressive methods as he exhorts the people to demand full restitution of tribunician rights (3.48=34). In the letter of Mithridates to the king of Parthia – perhaps the most famous of all these excerpts (4.69=67) – there speaks the voice of those in the path of Roman conquest, denouncing Roman greed and imperialism in terms that would set a precedent for the later words of the Samnite Herennius Pontius (Livy 9.1) and the Caledonian Calgacus (Tac. *Agr.* 30–2).[129] Finally, in its fearless, even threatening address to the senate, Pompey's letter captures his ambition, talent, and self-importance. His conclusion sums it up: *quod ego uos moneo quaesoque ut animaduortatis neu cogatis necessitatibus priuatim mihi consulere . . . relicui uos estis: qui nisi subuenitis, inuito et praedicente me exercitus hinc et cum eo omne bellum Hispaniae in Italiam transgradientur* (2.98=82.8, 10 'I strongly advise and request that you take thought for this matter and do not force me privately to consider my own needs. . . . You are our last hope: unless you help us, though I am unwilling and have already warned you, my army will cross into Italy and with it will come the whole Spanish war'). The combination of aggression and pleading in *moneo quaesoque* introduces the equally well chosen *cogatis* with which Pompey neatly subverts the real power relationships of the situation, claiming that any drastic action he might take will be forced on him – a theme that returns in the last sentence (*inuito et praedicente me*).[130] 'Privately' is an especially dangerous word in this context, echoing as it does the self-justifications of and accusations against late-republican strong men who marshalled private armies with private funds (e.g. Cic. *Off.* 1.25, Aug. *RG* 11, Suet. *Jul.* 24.2). But Pompey's power is felt most keenly in his warning that failure to help his army will bring war into Italy. His surface meaning is that when he is forced to bring his men home to feed off Italian land Sertorius' rebels will chase them over the Alps, an unrealistic claim but one which would strike fear into a senate who had earlier in this very letter been reminded of Hannibal's invasion of Italy, also from Spain (2.98=82.4). Underneath, however, is the threat that Pompey himself can invade Italy as Hannibal did – and will, if the senate refuses help.[131]

Though the means by which the individual voices are articulated differ, these long excerpts do share certain features, two of which are of particular interest. First, each speaker uses a calculated blend of irony and flattery to insult his opponent(s) and win his audience's support, carefully negotiating a stance of authority and trustworthiness. So Lepidus, for example, adopts a tentative and sympathetic tone to address the *populus*, repeatedly returning to the word *tutus* ('safe') to assure them that he understands their fears, which he claims are matched by his own anxieties about the republic. Establishing his authority as that of the statesman who can see clearly the good qualities of the plebs and the bad ones of Sulla's followers (the powerful *pauci*, 'few'), Lepidus first assures his listeners that he understands their reluctance to resort to violence; but his sympathy turns to exhortation as he points out that the tyrant Sulla, too, wants to be *tutus*, and can be so only by enslaving the *populus*. Since the oppressor can better safeguard his own than can the oppressed, the plebs must act now or never: Lepidus constructs the present as a time of extremes in which the people's fear must be turned outward in order to recover the safety and the freedom of which they have been robbed (1.55=48.10 'In these times one must be slave or master, one must fear or cause others to fear, Quirites'). Speaking to the senate, on the other hand, Philippus urges his fellow *patres* to oppose Lepidus' revolutionary plans. His authority comes from two sources: first his recognition, despite the lure of wishful thinking, of the reality of the present dangers with which he opens his speech (1.77=67.1 'I would most wish . . . but on the contrary . . .'); second, his affiliation with the few (*pauci*) who had seen the threat from Lepidus all along (§6). Having thus established his right to speak, he taunts the senate with their *metus* ('fear'), reminding them of Lepidus' violent measures and urging them to go on the attack to recover their liberty. In effect, his points are precisely the same as Lepidus'; it is his handling of his audience that is different, especially his treatment of their anxiety. Where Lepidus treads gently, associating his own fear with the plebs' and working to encourage them to act despite their worries, Philippus attacks the senate for cowardice, for trying to remain *tuti* where only boldness will help them. In conclusion, both speakers offer two options, the first patently unacceptable ('if you call Sulla's acts freedom, then stay as you are'; 'if you like revolution, go along with the traitors'), the second a call to defend their liberty ('rouse yourselves,

Quirites, and with the good help of the gods follow the consul Marcus Aemilius in recovering your liberty'; 'but if liberty and the truth please you more, pass decrees worthy of the name [of senate] and strengthen the brave spirit of your defenders').[132] But while Lepidus ends with a call to follow *him*, Philippus appends a final paragraph, couched in formal curial language, asking for due process in the passing of a *senatus consultum ultimum* (1.77=67.22).

This responsion between the two orations in Book 1 illustrates the second important feature shared by these passages. Despite the lack of a narrative matrix in which to site these *orationes* and *epistulae*, it seems clear that there were complex links among them of theme and in some cases of language. Like Lepidus and Philippus, Licinius explores the concepts of *tutum* and *metus* (cf. 3.48=34.3, 8, 21); likewise, though their words are not in formal responsion, the impetuous young Pompey's letter in some ways answers the aged consul Cotta (2.98=82.1 ~ 2.47=44.2, 4). This is a technique that is better visible in the *BJ*, in which two *populares*, Memmius and Marius, give orations that, though independent, nevertheless respond closely to each other (chh. 31 ~ 85); the technique is taken up by later historians, especially Livy (so the speeches of Canuleius, 4.3–5, and Appius Claudius Crassus, 6.40–1, are meant to be read as a pair, as are Claudius' speech and his own earlier exhortation, which opens Book 5).[133]

Ethnography: 'variety, instruction, and delight'[134]

It is not only Romans, however, in whom Sallust is interested in the *Historiae*. Since Herodotus, ancient history had accommodated the separate but closely related genre of ethnography, the study of foreign peoples. Herodotean excursuses on the Persians, Egyptians, and Scythians provide what François Hartog has called a mirror in which concepts of Greekness are reflected and analysed; the technique, as well as the fascination with other peoples, derives ultimately from Homer's *Odyssey*.[135] Cato incorporated Italian ethnography and geography into his *Origines*, which were in part an exploration of the founding of different Italian city-states, while in his monographs Sallust made Rome itself the object of the ethnographer's gaze.[136] While it is impossible now to evaluate the effect of the digressions on the narrative pace and structure of the *Historiae*, we can get a glimpse of Sallust's treatment of other worlds, especially Sardinia and Corsica

(2.1–13), the Black Sea area (3.62–80=43–59), and southern Italy and Sicily (4.23–9=19–25).[137]

The fragments show an interest in the shape of the country described, its mythological background, and the origin and names of its inhabitants. In most cases, the scholarly, often recondite information is linked to something easily understandable. Thus the shapes of Sardinia and Pontus are illustrated with reference to objects on a familiar scale (a human foot and a Scythian bow respectively);[138] when describing Pontus, Sallust does so as any traveller might, his systematic progress along the coast again making the strange more accessible.[139] Similar is his tracing of the mythology attaching to these places: figures such as Achilles, Jason and Medea, the Amazons, Daedalus, Hercules, and Scylla and Charybdis come into the discussion either as long-distant founding figures whose stories lie behind the historical period, or as myths that can now be domesticated with a 'scientific' explanation.[140] Finally, in discussing the inhabitants of these places, Sallust seems to have concentrated on their movements, especially in their founding migrations (e.g. 2.9=10, 3.68=48),[141] and on their names (e.g. 2.5=7, 3.70=50). Here the historian's impulse to familiarize the unfamiliar manifests itself as an interest in etymology and translation: the Balari were runaways (2.9: *balari* means 'fugitives' in the local language); the Euxine is nicknamed the 'unfriendly' (*inhospitale*, translating the Greek *axenos*: 3.67=47). In each of these areas, then, Sallust uses ethnogeography as way of introducing the rest of the world to Rome.

But ethnography serves another purpose as well. As Roman roads codified the routes of expansion and facilitated further conquest, so these geographical studies make textual inroads into foreign territories, accompanying Roman invasion – a technique familiar from other historians and probably beginning with Herodotus, whose ethnographies are situated, for the most part, at the point at which the invading forces reach a new country. Conventional ethnographical features like rivers (e.g. 3.72=52, 79–80=58–9) and climate (3.65–6=45–6) could serve the purposes of a tale of military conquest, as well, coming into the story when they are relevant for the topography of a campaign.[142] The interaction of narrative and narrated, of discourse and story, is especially crucial in a tale of empire, as scholars have recently stressed: by telling the story of conquest, an epic or historical narrative reinforces the extension and legitimization of temporal power. Cicero clearly recognized this, as witnessed by his argument for the diffusion of poetry about Roman *res gestae*: 'if our deeds are limited only by the regions of the world, we ought to desire that where our weapons penetrate, there our glory and our fame reach also, both because they are ennobling to those people whose history is being written, and because certainly for those who are fighting to the death for glory's sake this is the greatest encouragement for them to endure dangers and toils.'[143] It is possible that Sallust's ethnographies served a similar function, incorporating the strange into Rome's empire as Roman soldiers expanded its physical domain.

Foreign lands could also provide an escape, as they nearly do for the rebel Sertorius, in whose story Sallust evokes the mythical Isles of the Blest (1.100–3=89–92), including a reference to the human urge to see unknown things (1.103=89 *more humanae cupidinis ignara uisendi*) – the same urge that Metellus indulged at the dinner table, though there inappropriately. Their very strangeness was intrinsically appealing: hence the citing of the bizarre, such as the Scythians in their wagons (3.76=56, an ethnographical standby), or the fiercest natives in a region (3.74=54), or the poisonous plant that resembles balm, whose victims die with a grimace that looks like a smile (2.10=12). Here again, Sallust's ethnographic sections may have held a kind of lens up to Rome, showing it both the strange in the light of the familiar, and the strange on its own, either as a place of refuge or simply a source of *miracula*.[144]

NOTES

1. These present special problems of genre, being neither history in its technical sense (a *commentarius* was a set of notes, generally intended to provide a basis for a more elaborate narrative) nor in fact – at least in so far as the books by Caesar himself are concerned – proper *commentarii*: no one dared elaborate them, and both Hirtius, author of *De Bello Gallico* 8, and Cicero (*Brut.* 262), declared them perfect just as they were. For an introduction to the problems see P. T. Eden, 'Caesar's Style: intelligence versus inheritance', *Glotta* 40 (1962), 74–117; H. C. Gotoff, 'Towards a practical criticism of Caesar's prose style', *ICS* 9 (1984), 1–18; Conte (1994), 225–33 and C. Hammond, *Caesar: Seven Commentaries on the Gallic War* (Oxford, 1996), xi–xlvi.

2. The dates are traditional but probably roughly accurate (Syme (1964), 13–14); we do not know exactly when each monograph was published, though they predate the *Historiae*.

3. Sallust may have planned to extend it to 60 (Syme (1964), 191–2), or even as far as 40 (*RICH*, 117); Syme (1964), 179–80 and Rawson (1991), 546–69 have shown that there was a considerable 'archaeology' at the beginning that covered – perhaps in quite a sensational manner – the later career of the dictator Sulla. On the archaeologies in the monographs see below, n. 71.

4. Syme (1964), 256. Cf. Earl (1965), 237: 'Sallust's aim was . . . an exercise in morbid pathology'; R. F. Newbold determines that Sallust probably had a high level of diffuse anxiety ('Patterns of anxiety in Sallust, Suetonius, and Procopius,' *AHB* 4 (1991), 48). The prefaces have occasioned critics some difficulties at least since the time of Quintilian (first century A.D.; his criticism is at 3.8.9): on their form see below, n. 24 and Appendix.

5. *BC* 3.1; *BJ* 4.1–4; see further above, p. 14 and below, p. 52 on history as a replacement for political action.

6. C. Macleod, *Collected Essays* (Oxford, 1983), 68.

7. On his political moderation see Syme (1964), 116–17, 253–4, Conte (1994), 237–8.

8. The pervasive idea that history is both practically and morally useful goes back at least as far as Thucydides. One of his precursors makes a programmatic statement that well anticipates Sallust: *nam neque alacriores ad rem publicam defendundam neque segniores ad rem perperam faciundam annales libri commouere quosquam possunt* (Sempronius Asellio 2P, 'For annals can inspire no one either to be more eager to defend the state or to be slower to act wrongly'): the implication is that Asellio's own analytical history, which would explain not only what happened but also why, *could* do so. See also Oakley (1997), 73–4, and for a negative view of Sallust's 'harping' on the theme of morality and emphasis on the 'personalities of history' see M. L. W. Laistner, *The Greater Roman Historians* (Berkeley, 1947), 52–5.

9. *nam saepe ego audiui Q. Maxumum, P. Scipionem, ⟨alios⟩ praeterea ciuitatis nostrae praeclaros uiros solitos ita dicere, quom maiorum imagines intuerentur, uehementissume sibi animum ad uirtutem adcendi. scilicet non ceram illam neque figuram tantam uim in sese habere, sed memoria rerum gestarum eam flammam egregiis uiris in pectore crescere neque prius sedari quam uirtus eorum famam atque gloriam adaequauerit* (*BJ* 4.5–6). See Scanlon (1987), 17, 49–50, 80 n.29 and Paul (1984) ad loc.

10. Earl (1961), 28.

11. Earl (1961), 31, general discussion 18–40; there is an overview of Roman *uirtus* (in German) by W. Eisenhut, *Virtus Romana* (Munich, 1973). Marius' speech at *BJ* 85 is the clearest statement of this kind of self-made *uirtus* – though Marius himself fails to live up to the ideal.

12. On the prefaces and the reader's attention see Scanlon (as above, n. 9); on compromised *uirtus* see Syme (1964), 268–9 with Earl (1965), 237–8 and above, pp. 11, 27; on the *syncrisis* in the *BC* see above, p. 19.

13. It has been extensively argued that Sallust's pessimistic, critical mode, which Tacitus followed, was exceptional: *RICH*, e.g. 167–8.

14. On Coelius see bibliographical Appendix; for general remarks on monographs ('a new trend in Roman historiography': Forsythe (1994), 41) see Syme (1964), 57, G. Puccioni, *Il Problema della Monografia Storica Latina* (1981), and Scanlon (1987), 66–7. Conte (1994), 235–6 makes a plausible connection between Sallust's choice of the monograph form and the 'demand for short works in a refined style that had grown as the result of the neoteric experiment.'

15. Sketched at Leeman (1963), 87 (from whom come the descriptive tags quoted here) and Oakley (1997), 145. The third type, a 'somewhat heavy and elaborate chancery style' with frequent use of participles and indirect speech, will surface occasionally in Livy; it is especially noticeable in Caesar, and may derive ultimately from Polybius.

16. Goodyear, *CHCL* 2.269.

17. Gay (1974), 9, 189; for the ancient version of the same idea see especially Seneca, *Ep.* 114 (translated in D. A. Russell and M. Winterbottom, *Ancient Literary Criticism* (Oxford, 1972), 363–7). On the author's *persona* see the fundamental discussion of Booth (²1983).

18. This is an old topic that has come under much recent discussion, e.g. Plass (1988) and J. Henderson, 'Tacitus/The world in pieces,' in A. J. Boyle, ed., *The Imperial Muse: Flavian Epicist to Claudian* (Victoria, 1990), 167–210.

19. On Sallust and Thucydides see above, pp. 12, 16–18. Cic., *Brut.* 66 suggests an analogy between Cato (Sallust's Roman model) and Thucydides: 'this understandable but highly audacious connection largely determined the later course of Roman historiography' (Leeman (1963), 72).

20. There are many discussions of Sallust's style. Conte (1994), 241–2 is brief but good; McGushin (1977), 13–21 has much useful detail; the classic treatment is Syme (1964), 240–73.

21. For antithesis see McGushin (1977), 14, 17, Syme (1964), 265; for political jargon and the speeches' self-subversion see Syme (1964), 162–3, 198–201, 255–6.

22. The title is not certain. Reynolds (OCT) and Horsfall (1981), 107 prefer a version of *De Coniuratione Catilinae*; for a defence of *Bellum*, the term used also by Quintilian (3.8.9), see *RICH*, 147 n. 1.

23. The extent of the preface is controversial; for the view taken here see e.g. McGushin (1977), 291–2. The sketch of Catiline (5.1–8) is stated explicitly to precede the narrative (4.5 *initium narrandi*); and the digressive formula at 5.9 (esp. *supra repetere*) suggests that 6–13 is not part of the main narrative either. It might be argued that the sketch of Catiline continues no further than 5.5 and that the main narrative begins with *Hunc* (5.6: 'This man . . .'); but it seems odd to

leave the main narrative almost immediately and to launch into a long retrospective digression at 6–13.

24. It has been argued by D. C. Earl that Sallust, influenced by Aristotelian works which were 'rediscovered' at Rome during his lifetime, was aiming at a consciously 'philosophical' preface ('Prologue-form in ancient historiography', *ANRW* 1.2.842–56 (1972)).

25. As the preface progresses, it becomes clear that *silentio* = both 'without speaking' and 'without being spoken about' (A. J. Woodman, 'A note on Sallust, *Catilina* 1.1', *CQ* 23 (1973), 310).

26. The point, of course, is that *auctor* often = 'author (of a literary work)'.

27. Diodorus is often thought to be echoing the Hellenistic historian Duris. Although there is no guarantee of that (K. S. Sacks, *Diodorus Siculus and the First Century* (Princeton, 1990), 94–5), as early as the fifth century B.C. it was debated whether, or to what extent, language can describe 'reality' (see e.g. G. B. Kerferd, *The Sophistic Movement* (Cambridge, 1981), 80–2).

28. See e.g. Isoc. *Pan.* 13, Diod. 20.2.2, Liv. 6.20.8, Plin. *Ep.* 8.4.3; J. Diggle, '*Facta dictis aequare*', *PACA* 17 (1983), 59–60. Feeney (1994), however, translates the phrase as meaning 'deeds have to be made equal to words'.

29. See e.g. Isoc. *Plataicus* 4.

30. Sallust's manner of expressing his twofold difficulty evidently gave rise to criticism, against which he is defended in the second century A.D. by Gellius (4.15). For Tacitus' allusion to this passage of Sallust see p. 93.

31. The insertion of the sketch at this point is not arbitrary but, by revealing that he has retired from politics, is designed to prove that he is now free from partisanship and can thus write fairly, i.e. truthfully. See further *RICH*, 73–4.

32. *carptim* alludes to Sallust's chosen form of the monograph.

33. For the expulsion see Dio 40.63.4; Syme (1964), 33–4.

34. Dio 43.9.2; Syme (1964), 39.

35. Syme (1964), 270 also talks in terms of a 'conversion'.

36. The usual explanation of the passage is that Sallust had originally attempted to write history before being diverted into politics, but this seems incredibly lame and is not supported by what he himself says at 3.3. For the notion that the historian performs what he describes see esp. Liv. 10.31.10–15, Hor. *Odes* 2.1.18 (with Nisbet–Hubbard's n.).

37. See R. B. Rutherford, *The Meditations of Marcus Aurelius: a Study* (Oxford, 1989), 103–7.

38. See esp. R. Renehan, 'A traditional pattern of imitation in Sallust and his sources', *CP* 71 (1976), 100–1. It has recently been observed that in the ancient world describing oneself in terms of a famous predecessor 'is to be more, not less, oneself' (M. W. Gleason, *Making Men: Sophists and Self-Presentation in Ancient Rome* (Princeton, 1995), 154). It is of course well known that Sallust draws upon many earlier authors in his prefaces: see P. Perrochat, *Les Modèles grecs de Salluste* (Paris, 1949); for Plato in particular see also B. D. MacQueen, *Plato's Republic in the Monographs of Sallust* (Chicago, 1981).

39. *igitur* ('Therefore') makes it clear that the reference to truth is to be seen in terms of Sallust's departure from public life (above, n. 31).

40. Syme (1964), 268–9 has said that 'Sallust is in his own person a document of concentrated energy and controlled violence', that he 'betrays an insight verging on sympathy' for those whose energy is 'diverted into criminal paths', and that he has a 'keen interest in the psychology of ambition and violence'. Note also V. D'Huys, 'How to describe violence in historical narrative', *Anc. Soc.* 18 (1987), 211.

41. The sketch follows the standard pattern for describing someone's life: see below, p. 103 and n. 85.

42. For Sallust as an imitator of Thucydides see Sen. *Contr.* 9.1.13, Vell. 36.2, Quint. 10.1.101; Perrochat (above, n. 38), T. F. Scanlon, *The Influence of Thucydides on Sallust* (Heidelberg, 1980), and e.g. E. Keitel, 'The influence of Thucydides 7.61–71 on Sallust *Cat.* 20–21', *CJ* 82 (1987), 293–300. The scope of the retrospective digression starting at *BJ* 5.4 is controversial (see Paul (1984), 23–4); for *H.* see above, p. 41 n. 3.

43. This statement anticipates that of the emperor Verus writing to his friend and historian, Fronto: 'my achievements are of course as great as they are, whatever that is; but they will seem as great as you want them to seem' (Fronto 2.196); see also Plin. *Ep.* 7.33.10 (below, p. 102), and Woodman–Martin (1996) on Tac. *A.* 3.65.1.

44. This point seems not to be contradicted by Sallust's allegation that writers have exaggerated the achievements of Athens, an allegation which he uses as a foil to contrast the lack of writers to describe early Rome (8.5). It is this lack which he himself remedies in the present digression, and both here and in the main narrative it is taken for granted that he has not exaggerated (cf. 3.2, 4.3).

45. See Earl (1961) and *The Moral and Political Tradition of Rome* (London, 1967).

46. Cato 2P (= Cic. *Planc*. 66). Sallust's familiarity with Cato's work may be inferred from the frequency with which he was accused of pillaging its (by now archaic) vocabulary: see Suet. *Aug*. 86.3, *Gramm*. 15.2 with Kaster (1995), Quint. 8.3.29. There is a full study of Sallust's archaizing vocabulary in W. D. Lebek, *Verba Prisca* (Göttingen, 1970). On Sallust's style see further above, pp. 11–13.

47. *Letter to Pompey* 3, *Thuc*. 15, 41; see *RICH*, 40–3.

48. See e.g. Earl (1961), 86, Syme (1964), 66–7 and n. 34.

49. For the various scandalous stories surrounding Catiline see D. H. Berry, *Cicero Pro P. Sulla Oratio* (Cambridge, 1996), 277–8.

50. For such superlative expressions elsewhere see Woodman–Martin (1996) on Tac. *A*. 3.11.2 or Woodman (1983) on Vell. 71.1; they are esp. common in Thucydides and Livy. This is one of only two passages in *BC* where Sallust refers to his own experience of events (the other is 48.9, but cf. also 53.6); the digression thereby introduced 'occupies the precise centre of the monograph' (Syme (1964), 68).

51. At 31.1 *permoueri* is evidently used for the simple *moueri* (which occurs in the same image at *BJ* 41.10) but *facies* (*OLD* 2a, 7) makes the metaphor clear (see e.g. Tac. *A*. 4.67.2 *antequam Vesuuius mons ardescens faciem loci uerteret*). At 36.5 both *uis* (*OLD* 9b) and *inuado* (*OLD* 4a) are technical of disease. At 38.1 *exagitare* (*OLD* 1da) and *incendere* (*OLD* 1d) allude to the common image of a torch (*OLD fax* 8a), which in this case has evidently been smouldering before being shaken into life. Sallust was well known for his metaphors (Suet. *Gramm*. 10.6 with Kaster (1995) here and on 10.2); see also E. Skard, 'Die Bildersprache des Sallust', *Serta Eitremiana* (Oslo, 1942), 141–64.

52. Granius Licinianus 36A–B (p. 59 Camozzi).

53. See also *RICH*, 124–7.

54. It is no doubt this oddity which has led some commentators to say that *bene dicere* is not to be taken with *rei publicae*.

55. At 3.2 it is implied that some historians will (have) criticize(d): this point, which is interestingly modelled on Pericles' speech of praise at Thuc. 2.35.2 and seems designed as a foil for the more extensive remarks on praise which follow, presumably constitutes an implied defence of what Sallust himself is about to do in *BC*.

56. It is not unreasonable to assume that Sallust had read Cicero's letter: see *RICH*, 149 n. 30.

57. See Syme (1964), 105–11 for Sallust's treatment of Cicero and scholarly reaction thereto.

58. For similar inhibitions see Liv. 45.25.3, Tac. *A*. 15.63.3; in general Brock (1995), esp. 212–13.

59. See D. C. Innes, '*Quo usque tandem patiemini?*', *CQ* 27 (1977), 468.

60. Embedded within this introduction is a brief summary of an earlier debate: see S. J. Heyworth and A. J. Woodman, 'Sallust, *Bellum Catilinae* 50.3–5', *LCM* 11 (1986), 11–12 (reading the transmitted *dixerat* at 50.4).

61. It is these two speeches which account for the extraordinarily high percentage of direct speech (almost 27%) in *BC* (the other speeches are at 20.2–17, 33, 35 [a letter] and 58). This percentage is significantly higher than that for any other ancient historical work apart from that of Dionysius of Halicarnassus: this statistic seems appropriate in a monograph whose author argues for the importance of *dicere* as opposed to *facere* (pp. 13–17), though it is ironical that in the four major speeches the speaker is made to cast doubt on the effectiveness of words (20.15, 51.10, 52.35, 58.1). If the above percentage is added to the amount of space devoted to the preface (1–13), it emerges that almost half the monograph is given over to things other than a narrative of the actual events of the Catilinarian conspiracy.

62. For a survey of views see McGushin (1977), 309–11; add W. W. Batstone, 'The antithesis of virtue: Sallust's *synkrisis* and the crisis of the late Republic', *CA* 7 (1988), 1–29.

63. See e.g. A. T. Wilkins, *Villain or Hero: Sallust's Portrayal of Catiline* (New York, 1994), 29–70, 131–7, adducing other parallels in addition to those mentioned here.

64. Cicero in fact attacks Catiline for the very qualities which he shares with Caesar (*Cat*. 1.26

labores tui . . . uigilare, 3.16 *uigilaret, laboraret*). It is noteworthy that, while Sallust condemns Catiline for aiming at monarchy (5.6 *regnum*), he nowhere associates monarchy with Caesar, the most famous and most recent individual to be charged with this aim.

65. Syme (1964), 58. See also Earl (1961), 85–6.

66. Earl (1961), 95; cf. Syme (1964), 68 'a fierce and fraudulent oration'.

67. For such activities see Woodman (1983) on Vell. 79.1, 85.4, (1977) on 114.1–3; Kraus (1994), 351 (Index). On good generals see also A. M. Eckstein, *Moral Vision in the 'Histories' of Polybius* (Berkeley, 1995), 161–93.

68. For the second-person subjunctive as a means of achieving vividness see [Long.] *Subl.* 26; K. Gilmartin, 'A rhetorical figure in Latin historical style', *TAPA* 105 (1975), 99–121, drawing attention to the unusualness of the present passage (p. 116).

69. For the significance of frontal wounds see *BJ* 85.29; I. M. Le M. DuQuesnay in *AA*, 67 and n. 58.

70. See e.g. McGushin (1977), 287, who is nevertheless sceptical of the notion, or Scanlon (1987), 34–5.

71. It is possible that in thus selecting several beginnings he is imitating Polybius, whose 'main' history begins in 220 B.C. (1.3.2, 4.2.1) but who identifies other starting points at 387/6 (the beginning of Roman naval power: 1.6, 1.12) and 264–60 (the first time the Romans crossed by sea from Italy: 1.5). Both writers are ultimately influenced by the Thucydidean pattern of archaeology + brief history of the immediate past (the *pentecontaetia*) + main narrative; see also (above), nn. 3, 42, and Feeney (1994).

72. For the history of the idea see Paul (1984) on 41.2 and W. V. Harris, *War and Imperialism in Republican Rome, 327–70 B.C.* (Oxford, 1985), 127–8, 266–7; for the *Historiae* see below, n. 103.

73. On the monograph form see also n. 14.

74. Though, paradoxically, Catiline is not present in Rome, nor in the narrative, for fully one half of the *BC* (he departs at 32.1, writes a letter at 34.2–35, but is not seen again until the battle of Pistoria, 56–61). For the 'neat dramatic arc' of the *BC* see Scanlon (1987), 63; for Jugurtha's person see Levene (1992), 54.

75. For the considerable difficulties with Sallust's chronologies see Syme (1964), 142–7; Paul (1984) on 37.3 and 43.1.

76. Domestic affairs are depicted primarily in what Scanlon calls 'reaction narratives,' scenes at Rome in which the populace and the nobles react to what has happened in Africa (Scanlon (1988), 143–4). These are much more frequent before Metellus takes command (20 OCT pages out of 37 as opposed to eight OCT pages out of 69), a pattern noticed by Earl (1961), 70.

77. For extended discussion see Levene (1992). The introduction of Caesar and Cato in the *BC* has a similar, though less obvious, effect.

78. The great German historian Mommsen, for example, called it a 'lionhunt'; see also Paul (1984), 19–20 and 264–8.

79. The fundamental discussion is that of Scanlon (1988); see also T. Wiedemann, 'Sallust's *Jugurtha*: Concord, discord, and the digressions', *G&R* 40 (1993), 48–57.

80. I will argue this fully in 'Jugurthine disorder,' to appear in a collection of articles on historiography (Leiden, 1998); on Jugurtha the hero see also J.-M. Classen, 'Sallust's Jugurtha – Rebel or freedom fighter? On crossing crocodile-infested waters', *CW* 86 (1993), 273–97.

81. There is a large bibliography on the structure of the *BJ*, much of it in German; for references see Syme (1964), 141 n. 4 and Scanlon (1988), 144–6.

82. On bribery in this period see Paul (1984), 261–3; on money and exchange as symptomatic of slipping categories see S. von Reden, 'Deceptive readings: poetry and its value reconsidered', *CQ* 45 (1995), 47–8 and Barthes (1975), 1–22.

83. On the opposition of the *noui* to the *nobiles* in Sallust see Earl (1961), 32–5; for the larger issues involved see the dicussions of Wiseman (1971) and P. A. Brunt, '*Nobilitas* and *nouitas*', *JRS* 72 (1982), 1–22.

84. On Marius' election and Sallust's misleading report of his early career – the historian suggests that he had an easy time of it, whereas in fact his rise had been slow and difficult – see Earl (1965), 235 and Paul (1984) on 63.5; on Marius see now R. J. Evans, *Gaius Marius: a Political Biography* (Pretoria, 1994).

85. On Marius' reforms see L. Keppie, *The Making of the Roman Army: from Republic to Empire*

(1984), 57–79 and J. W. Rich, 'The supposed Roman manpower shortage of the later second century B.C.', *Historia* 32 (1983), 323–30; on his affinities with Jugurtha see Earl (1961), 75 and n. 1, Scanlon (1987), 49 and below, n. 93.

86. On Servius Tullius as a *nouus homo* see Wiseman (1971), 109; for Servius and Marius as exemplifying changes of fortune from humble to high, cf. Val. Max 3 4 ('Concerning those who have turned out to be famous though coming from a low station': Servius is in §3) and 6.9.14 ('that Marius, who was such a low inhabitant of Arpinum'). Marius was a conventional example of the power of *fortuna*: see T. F. Carney, *A Biography of C. Marius* (Assen, 1961), 5.

87. Sallust prefaces the character sketch by saying that Sisenna, in whose *Historiae* the dictator figured, had described his subject 'with an insufficiently free voice,' that is, not critically enough (95.2); Sallust himself suggests that he too would be deterred from writing about Sulla's later career ('for as to what he did later, I am unsure whether it would cause me more shame or more revulsion to recount it,' 95.4). Sulla, of course, wrote his own history in the form of an autobiography, which Sallust used as a source; on Sulla in Sallust's *Historiae* see above, n. 3.

88. *Per idem tempus aduorsum Gallos ab ducibus nostris Q. Caepione et Cn. Mallio male pugnatum. quo metu Italia omnis contremuerat. illique et inde usque ad nostram memoriam Romani sic habuere, alia omnia uirtuti suae prona esse, cum Gallis pro salute, non pro gloria certare. sed postquam bellum in Numidia confectum et Iugurtham Romam uinctum adduci nuntiatum est, Marius consul absens factus est et ei decreta prouincia Gallia, isque Kalendis Ianuariis magna gloria consul triumphauit. et ea tempestate spes atque opes ciuitatis in illo sitae* (114).

89. On the ending see Levene (1992), 54–5; on double closures see Fowler (1989), 98–100; more on closure below, n. 91.

90. Though Levene rightly emphasizes that we are told neither of Jugurtha's presence in the triumph nor of his death.

91. On *spes* ('hope, expectation') in the *BJ* see Scanlon (1987), 37–61. On the narrative effect of the ending cf. Barthes (1975), 76: 'Expectation thus becomes the basic condition for truth: truth, these narratives tell us, is what is *at the end* of expectation. This design . . . implies a return to order, for expectation is a disorder: disorder is supplementary, it is what is forever added on without solving anything, without finishing anything; order is complementary, it completes, fills up, saturates, and dismisses everything that risks adding on: truth is what completes, what closes.' Jugurtha is one manifestation of disorder, which ultimately infects even the form of the narrative itself.

92. Syme (1964), 138, 268–9. While Sallust himself does not credit Jugurtha with *uirtus*, both Micipsa and Scipio are sure he has it (6.2, 7.2, 9.2–3, 10.2, 8), and Sallust does not contradict them. While Marius' *uirtus* is nowhere vouched for by the authorial voice and is attested by less reliable sources – e.g. Marius himself (85.32) and his soldiers (92.2) – in mentioning characteristics that often accompany it (energy, integrity, etc.) the sketch at 63.2–3 implies his *uirtus*.

93. On Marius and Jugurtha at Numantia see Paul (1984), 5, 31–2. On Marius' likeness to Jugurtha compare also 63.6 (Marius will rush headlong, *praeceps*) ~ 8.2 (Jugurtha warned against rushing *praeceps*); and 64.2 (Metellus warns Marius not to 'seek from the Roman people that which was denied him by law' – i.e. the consulate) ~ 8.2 (Scipio warns Jugurtha that 'it is dangerous to buy from the few that which belongs to the many' – i.e. power).

94. Because it is restricted in the narrative to the digressions – the parts of the text that are off the main road, as it were – Carthage does not cause the chaos that Jugurtha does, a composite creature fully participant in the narrative proper. On the effect produced by composite entities, beings in which normally distinct qualities are freely mingled or interchanged, cf. Barthes (1975), 215: 'it is fatal, the text [Balzac's *Sarrasine*] says, to remove the dividing line, the paradigmatic slash mark which permits meaning to function (the wall of the Antithesis), life to reproduce (the opposition of the sexes), property to be protected (rule of contract). In short the story *represents* . . . a generalized collapse of economies: the economy of language, usually protected by the separation of opposites, the economy of genders (the neuter must not lay claim to the human), the economy of the body (its parts cannot be interchanged, the sexes cannot be equivalent), the economy of money. . . . This catastrophic collapse always takes the same form: that of an unrestrained metonymy. By abolishing the paradigmatic barriers, this metonymy abolishes the power of *legal substitution* on which meaning is based: it is then no longer possible regularly to contrast opposites . . . it is no longer possible to safeguard an order of just equivalence; in a word, it is no longer possible to *represent*, to make things *representative*, individuated, separate, assigned.'

95. *Postea Phoenices . . . . Hipponem Hadrumetum Leptim aliasque urbis in ora maritima condidere . . . nam de Carthagine silere melius puto quam parum dicere, quoniam alio properare tempus monet* (19.1–2). Hannibal and the Carthaginians are mentioned earlier, at the very start of the war narrative (5.4 *dux Carthaginiensium Hannibal . . . uictis Carthaginiensibus*): the whole narrative is thus under the sign of the destroyed Carthage. In a paper delivered at the Classical Association AGM (Nottingham, April 1996) Ellen O'Gorman investigated some further implications of the presence of Carthage in Sallust's narrative, including the use of the city as a boundary.

96. *Igitur ad Catabathmon, qui locus Aegyptum ab Africa diuidit, secundo mari prima Cyrene est . . . ac deinceps duae Syrtes interque eas Leptis, deinde Philaenon arae, quem locum Aegyptum uorsus finem imperi habuere Carthaginienses, post aliae Punicae urbes* (19.3).

97. *Ita cum potentia auaritia sine modo modestiaque inuadere, polluere et uastare omnia, nihil pensi neque sancti habere, quoad semet ipsa praecipitauit . . . moueri ciuitas et dissensio ciuilis quasi permixtio terrae oriri coepit* (41.9–10). See also above, n. 51.

98. The digression itself marks the centre of one large-scale chiastically arranged structure extending from the battle of the Muthul up to a skirmish near Cirta (48–99: Scanlon (1988), 146–61; on the digression, 161–7). Just as Lepcis is introduced into the narrative by its request for help in maintaining its own political stability, so the story it triggers, forming the centre of a textual unit, appropriately tells of the imposition of form on chaos. On further structural implications and on the literary history of such anecdotes see Paul (1984) on 79.1.

99. The connection between the two is underscored by the fact that Jugurtha is the great-nephew of Masinissa, a Roman ally against Carthage during the war against Hannibal; Numidia's loyalty had remained fixed since that conflict but all surety was removed by Masinissa's death, probably in 148 B.C. (5.5). Even on the personal level of the Numidian royal house, then, connection with Carthage produces a reliable universe in which friends are friends and enemies, enemies.

100. Syme (1964), 179 (tempered optimism: Goodyear, *CHCL* 2.269); P. A. Brunt, 'On historical fragments and epitomes', *CQ* 30 (1980), 494 with his remarks about the importance of distinguishing between direct quotation (rare) and paraphrase (common) of an ancient author, and on the way the accidents of preservation can materially skew our impressions of a work.

101. McGushin (1992), 5–10 gives an account of the transmission of the *Historiae*; for Sallust and Plutarch see Syme (1964), 178.

102. McGushin (1992), 14 detects a further, Thucydidean division of the campaigning season into winter and summer. Reconstruction of the shape of the whole is problematic. The most recent attempt (of McGushin) follows a strictly chronological scheme; in response see the reviews by J. W. Rich in *CR* 43 (1993), 280–2 and 46 (1996), 250–1. On the 'archaeology' in Book 1 see above, n. 3.

103. We cannot say for certain, as Syme did, that no such digression on contemporary politics existed (Earl (1965), 236); if it did, the point of view expressed may have been broader than in the monographs, as shown e.g. by his less optimistic view of the period before 146 which takes account of the Struggle of the Orders: see McGushin (1992), 74–84, esp. 78–9.

104. For discussion of these conventions see bibliographical Appendix and D. den Hengst, *The Prefaces in the Historia Augusta* (Amsterdam 1981). See also above, p. 10 on the prologues to *BC* and *BJ*. A discussion of the prefatory fragments by T. F. Scanlon ('Reflexivity and irony in the Proem to Sallust's *Historiae*') is forthcoming in *Studies in Latin Literature and Roman History VII*, ed. C. Deroux (Brussels, 1997).

105. *Historiae, res gestae*, and *annales* may all refer to both title and contents; on titles see Horsfall (1981), 105–6. L. Calpurnius Piso Frugi (consul 133 B.C.) may have been the first to write *annales* in Latin (Forsythe (1994), 42).

106. On Sallust's end point see above, n. 3; for similar gestures in opening sentences cf. Livy 6.1.3 *ac deinceps*, Tac. *A.* 1.1.3 *et cetera*. The monographs' announced subjects are more neatly delineated (*BC* 4.3 *de Catilinae coniuratione*; *BJ* 5.1–2, *bellum . . . quod populus Romanus cum Iugurtha rege Numidarum gessit*), though the *BJ* deliberately inscribes itself into a larger context (above, p. 21).

107. The consuls, whose names are couched in the asyndetic form traditional in Roman dates, may be read not as individuals but as simply indicating Sallust's starting-point: so the fourth-century scholar Donatus, who discussed this line in his commentary on Verg. *Aen.* 1.1, compares *res* and *populus R.*, the subject and actor of the *Historiae*, with Vergil's *arma uirumque*. Sallust is quoting

Cato here, from the opening of his *Origines* (1P): *si ques homines sunt quos delectat populi Romani gesta discribere.*

108. On the kinship between epic and history see e.g. Wiseman (1979), 145–51, Fornara (1983) s.v. 'Homer' (Index) and D. C. Feeney, *The Gods in Epic* (Oxford, 1992), 42–5, 260–64; on Herodotus and Odysseus see I. L. Moles, 'Herodotus warns the Athenians', *PLLS* 9 (1996), 264–6, and on others see Walbank (1972), 51–2 and J. Marincola, 'Odysseus and the Historians', *Histos* (23 October 1996).

109. Sallust himself used a hexameter rhythm at *BJ* 5.1 (see Paul (1984) ad loc.); other examples of rhythmical openings are Livy *Praef.* 1 *Facturusne operae pretium sim* (cf. Quint. 9.4.74), Augustus, *RG* 1.1 *Rerum gestarum diui Augusti quibus orbem,* Tacitus, *A.* 1.1.1 *Vrbem Romam a principio reges habuere.* Scholars have been divided on whether these rhythms are deliberate; see Moles (1993), 157 with n. 77.

110. On Livy's *persona* see below, pp. 70–4. The basic treatment of writers' struggles with their precursors is H. Bloom, *The Anxiety of Influence* (New York, 1973); for classical authors see Thomas (1986).

111. Herkommer (1968) has 14 pages of examples, both Greek and Latin (137–51); on the claim see also above, p. 14. Tac. *A.* 1.1.3 *quorum causas procul habeo* is a quotation from Sallust: see A. J. Woodman, 'The preface to Tacitus' *Annals*: more Sallust?', *CQ* 42 (1992), 567–8.

112. On character see Walker (1952), 204–43, and C. Pelling, ed., *Characterization and Individuality in Greek Literature* (Oxford, 1990), esp. C. Gill on 'The character-personality distinction' (1–31); on character in ancient historiography and biography see A. Wallace-Hadrill, *Suetonius* (London, 1983), 8–22 (on the distinction between the two genres), 142–74. Some histories put less emphasis on the actions of individuals: Cato famously did not name many of his actors, presumably to underscore their importance as parts of the whole. On the *longue durée*, a term coined by F. Braudel to describe the passage of geographical time, a stretch over which long-term historical tendencies and developments can be observed, see P. Burke, 'Fernand Braudel' in J. Cannon, ed., *The Historian at Work* (London, 1980), 192.

113. The distinction was originally formulated by I. Bruns in 1898; independent and more accessible is S. Rimmon-Kenan, *Narrative Fiction: Contemporary Poetics* (London, 1983), 59–70 (with examples); on characterization through appearance, etc. see T. Barton, 'The *inventio* of Nero: Suetonius,' in J. Elsner and J. Masters, edd., *Reflections of Nero: Culture, History & Representation* (London, 1994), 57. For an overview of character(s) in the *Historiae* see Syme (1964), 195–6, 207–13.

114. Comprehensive discussion by Pomeroy (1991).

115. *in ulteriorem Hispaniam . . . regressus magna gloria concurrentium undique . . . uisebatur. . . . eum . . . ultra Romanum ac mortalium etiam morem curabant, exornatis aedibus per aulaea et insignia, scaenisque ad ostentationem histrionum fabricatis; simul croco sparsa humus et alia in modum templi celeberrimi. praeterea tum sedenti transenna demissum Victoriae simulacrum cum machinato strepitu tonitruum coronam capiti imponebat, tum uenienti ture quasi deo supplicabatur. toga picta plerumque amiculo erat accumbenti, epulae uero quaesitissimae, neque per omnem modo prouinciam, sed trans maria ex Mauretania uolucrum et ferarum incognita antea plura genera. quis rebus aliquantam partem gloriae dempserat, maxime apud ueteres et sanctos uiros superba illa, grauia, indigna Romano imperio aestimantis.*

116. Gowers (1993), 18: 'Writing against luxurious food and the superfluous desires of the body can now be explained as the most immediate and universally intelligible image of Rome's expansion.'

117. On the fascination the Romans felt for forbidden displays see C. A. Barton, *The Sorrows of the Ancient Romans* (Princeton, 1993).

118. The *toga picta* was the official garment of triumphing generals and worn only during the triumph or by special decree (Pompey was permitted by a decree of 63 to wear it in the Circus, a licence he exercised only once according to Vell. 40.4); on the connection between food and triumphs see Gowers (1993), 37, 39.

119. For general discussions see Plass (1988) and P. Sinclair, *Tacitus the Sententious Historian* (Pennsylvania, 1995).

120. The *Historiae* also contained apparently straightforward judgments (though their epigrammatic twist might have been lost in transmission or excerption), both favourable (e.g. 2.37=36, possibly on Appius Claudius: 'a serious man and in no pursuit (*ars*) inferior') and not (e.g. 4.73=77, probably of Lucullus and echoing *BC* 5.1 on Catiline: 'out of control and overweening').

121. The phrase 'loaded alternative' comes from D. Whitehead, *Latomus* 38 (1979), 474–95; see now also P. Sinclair, 'Rhetorical generalizations in Annales 1–6', *ANRW* 2.33.4.2795–2831 (1991) and below, p. 116 n. 82. Rumours can be exploited for similar purposes (see Martin – Woodman (1994) on Tac. *A*. 4.10–11): the example from book 4 discussed below combines both techniques (the lack of any named source implies a rumour).

122. That the device was an essential element of historiographical characterization is seen from Cic. *De orat.* 2.63, who in discussing the need to explain motivation suggests a choice among *casus, sapientia*, and *temeritas* (accident, wisdom, or rashness).

123. Plass (1988), 62–4 on the unexpected; for the abrupt epigrammatic style cf. Sen. *Ep*. 114.

124. On the *magis-quam* and *nisi* epigrams see Kraus (1994) on Livy 6.10.9, 6.20.14; for snide use of *alia* cf. also *H*. 1.116=110.

125. McGushin (1992), 158–9; also the items in n. 113 above.

126. On these activities see Paul (1984) ad loc.

127. 'Like Thucydides, Sallust uses speeches to provide a variation in narrative method; in each of his works speeches and letters . . . highlight the background and the atmosphere of important events and decisions. . . . By using the words of men who play an important role in the events he is dealing with, [he] is able to present a deeper and more varied analysis of the political and social problems which form the essence of his theme' (McGushin (1992), 14). On Dio Cassius see E. Gabba, 'The historians and Augustus', in Millar – Segal (1990), 70–1.

128. Syme (1964), 200 holds that Sallust's Cotta, the consul of 75, speaks in a way that 'conforms admirably' to the picture of him at Cic. *Brut*. 202: 'a plain unadorned style . . . neat and intelligent.'

129. See in general Balsdon (1979), 161–92, esp. 182–5. Accommodating anti-Roman sentiment in Roman historiography can be seen as yet another gesture of imperialism, a form of what has been called 'imperialist nostalgia' (Miles (1995), 175).

130. Not an uncommon argument, especially from men in power claiming to have unpopular actions forced on them; in a Sallustian-influenced text cf., for example, Livy 6.15.5–6, 38.7, 40.6. *Cogere*, which also appears frequently in the context of literary patronage, has been described as 'the *mot juste* for official encouragement' (C. O. Brink, *Horace on Poetry: Prolegomena to the Literary Epistles* (Cambridge, 1963), 191 n. 3); see J. Griffin, 'Augustus and the poets', in Millar – Segal (1990), 189–218 and now P. White, *Promised Verse* (Cambridge, Ma./London, 1993), 64–91 with the reservations of A. Cameron, *Callimachus and his Critics* (Princeton, 1995), 454–93.

131. For a contemporary equation of Caesar's and Hannibal's actions cf. Cic. *Att*. 7.11.1 '*Cingulum*' inquit '*nos tenemus, Anconem amisimus; Labienus discessit a Caesare.*' *utrum de imperatore populi Romani an de Hannibale loquimur?* It is a comparison that later writers, especially Lucan, make freely.

132. *adeste Quirites, et bene iuuantibus diuis M. Aemilium consulem . . . sequimini ad recipiundam libertatem* (1.55=48.27); *sin libertas et uera magis placent, decernite digna nomine et auge ingenium uiris fortibus* (1.77=67.20–1).

133. Sallust's speeches also echo orations in other authors: a good example is Philippus, who borrows from Cicero's *Philippics* (Syme (1964), 221–2). For more on intertextuality see below, p. 65 (and n. 59) and pp. 97–103 (and n. 47).

134. Syme (1964), 193.

135. For an over-schematic but useful introduction to ethnography in historiography see Fornara (1983), 12–16; on Herodotus see F. Hartog, *The Mirror of Herodotus* (Berkeley, 1988), D. Lateiner, *The Historical Method of Herodotus* (Toronto, 1989), 145–62; on Homer and ethnography see E. Hall, *Inventing the Barbarian* (Oxford, 1989), 52–3. One should emphasize that the ethnographical impulse is inseparable from the historical one: see esp. H. Immerwahr, *Form and Thought in Herodotus* (Cleveland 1966), 314–26 and D. Lowenthal, *The Past is a Foreign Country* (Cambridge, 1985). There is a new Italian monograph on ethnography in Sallust: R. Oniga, *Sallustio e l'Etnografia* (Pisa, 1995).

136. Cato: A. E. Astin, *Cato the Censor* (Oxford, 1978), 212–13, 216–18, 227–30; Sallust: Scanlon (1988), 138–43. On the importance to ethnographers of foreign institutions and 'moral oddity or aberration' (staples of Sallust on Rome) see Thomas (1982), 4.

137. That so many fragments from these sections have been preserved may testify only to the preoccupations of Sallust's ancient readers: but it is equally possible that their abundance points to the historian's own interests. (By comparison, there are very few traces of Livy's ethnography of

Carthage from Book 16, or of Gaul and Germany from Books 103–4.) Sallust may also have written ethnographies of Mesopotamia (4.61=62, 72=71, 78=75) and of Africa: Syme (1964), 193–5. On Rome and the barbarian see in general Balsdon (1979) and Y. Dauge, *Le Barbare* (Brussels, 1981).

138. On this standard way of describing the shape of countries see Thomas (1982), 3 with n. 12.

139. The first writer known to us to have produced such a systematic description – intended to accompany his map of the inhabited world – was the Ionian Hecataeus at the turn of the fifth century B.C. (Pearson (1939), 17–19, 28–31, 34–96); on travellers' tales and history see Gabba (1981), 60–2 and Fornara (1983), 13.

140. Hecataeus was again a pioneer, writing a genealogy of the gods and heroes that tied them to historical times and probably rationalized the myths (Pearson (1939), 96–106); see Fornara (1983), 4–12 on genealogy and history.

141. On nomadism/migration in ethnographies see Thomas (1982), 4, 23–4 and B. D. Shaw, '"Eaters of flesh, drinkers of milk": the ancient Mediterranean ideology of the pastoral nomad', in *Rulers, Nomads, and Christians in Roman North Africa* (Aldershot 1995), VI.5–31 (orig. published 1982–3).

142. Thomas (1982), 4–5; on ethnography as an introduction to conquered foreign lands see Wiseman (1979), 160 and n. 39; for the conventional features see Thomas (1982) s.vv. 'rivers, springs, etc.' and 'climate' (Index).

143. *si res eae quas gessimus orbis terrae regionibus definiuntur, cupere debemus, quo hominum nostrorum tela peruenerint, eodem gloriam famamque penetrare, quod cum ipsis populis de quorum rebus scribitur haec ampla sunt, tum eis certe qui de uita gloriae causa dimicant hoc maximum et periculorum incitamentum est et laborum (Arch. 23).* On empire and narrative see D. Quint, *Epic and Empire* (Princeton, 1993).

144. The desire for the strange or exotic can also serve imperialist urges, as at Tac. *Agr.* 10.4 *incognitas . . . insulas . . . inuenit domuitque. dispecta est et Thule. . . .* On the themes of escapism, utopias, and the miraculous see Gabba (1981), 53, 58–60 and Thomas (1982), 21–2.

III. LIVY

Memoria rerum gestarum (literally, 'memory of deeds') is yet another way of saying 'history', in the sense both of 'collective memory, tradition' and of 'history-writing.'[1] Memory and time are important concepts in all three of the major historians whom we are treating, but perhaps most for Livy, whose history must have consumed all of his working life[2] and, when intact, spanned the period from the sack of Troy through to the writer's own day. He signals the importance of time from the start of his preface, which was published together with the first unit of his history: *Facturusne operae pretium sim si a primordio urbis res populi Romani perscripserim nec satis scio nec, si sciam, dicere ausim . . . utcumque erit, iuuabit tamen rerum gestarum memoriae principis terrarum populi pro uirili parte et ipsum consuluisse* (*Praef.* 1, 3, 'Whether I will do something worthwhile if I write a detailed record of the deeds of the Roman people from the origin of the city I do not really know nor, if I knew, would I dare to say so . . . However that may be, it will nevertheless please me to have taken thought, to the best of my ability, for the history of the greatest nation in the world'). The tenses of the sentences quoted (*facturus . . . sim, erit, iuuabit*) put Livy's own potential literary achievement and resulting profit firmly in the future: this preface looks ahead, towards the moment of publication and beyond, to the reaction readers will have to his book. Yet the force of the past is felt here, as well: it is memory (*memoria rerum gestarum*) with which Livy concerns himself, and that concern is imagined as having already happened (the perfect infinitive *consuluisse*): the preface is written as if from the simultaneous vantage points of one looking ahead and of one looking back on a task already completed.

As he continues, however, it is clear that the present has an ambiguous status in Livy's thought, a status which is perhaps most easily understood if we contrast his treatment of it with those of his most famous precursor and successor. In Tacitus, the present represents a safe place from which the writer and his readers can look back on political dangers safely negotiated: it is the *felicitas temporum* ('good fortune of the times', *Agr.* 3.1) in which one can speak – and write – what one feels. It is also a time which Tacitus promises one day to celebrate in his history (*H.* 1.1.4). Instead, of course, he famously keeps moving backwards, away from the present, into the dark and corrupt past: each work (*Histories* – *Annals*) moves farther away from the emperors Nerva and Trajan under whom Tacitus lived and worked (see below, pp. 89–92). For Sallust, on the contrary, the present is a time of deep corruption and disappointment: political and social institutions alike are rotting away and preferment goes only to those who do not deserve it (*BC* 10.6, 11.3; *BJ* 3.1, 4.4). On the other hand, Sallust's own personal present is also a time of safety and retirement: he has withdrawn from politics and so, like Tacitus, is in a place from which he can survey the past in relative security. With Sallust's help his readers will similarly be able to step back from contemporary corruption and learn the salutary lessons that he claims his history will provide (*BJ* 4).

Livy's present is more Sallustian than Tacitean. Like the earlier historian, he implicitly claims early on that his work will benefit the state: the verb with which he describes what he does (*consuluisse*) is the same with which the Romans regularly describe what magistrates do – particularly consuls, whose title derives from their 'taking thought for', or 'consulting', the state.[3] Like Sallust, too, Livy withdraws from this present; but rather than retiring from contemporary politics to write about them, in the early books he has turned away to study the past (*Praef.* 5 *prisca illa*). His readers, in contrast, less interested in ancient history, hasten toward the present (4 *festinantibus ad haec noua*); hence his elaborate and careful defence, in this preface, of the utility and the pleasure to be derived from the study of the ancient past.[4] For, as the preface continues, we learn that history is *salubre ac frugiferum*, healthy and fruitful (10), medicine for the *res publica* in its present sickness. The usefulness, however, will come from Livy's own and his readers' contemplation of the past, which through a fall in discipline has itself been in a process of decline from an ancient – unspecified – time of health and expansion to Livy's own day, in which the Romans can bear neither their diseases nor their cures (9).[5] The preface, then, offers us a more complex picture of the past, present, and future, and of the relationship between writer and reader, than is offered by either Sallust's or Tacitus' work: it is a complicated mix of focuses, Livy's seemingly contradictory desires being both to escape from the here-and-now and to fix contemporary ills by confronting the past. History and the future come together in the troubled present: only by means of memory can the present – and by implication the future, the time both of publication and of reading – be cured; only by understanding the past can his readers hope to escape the cycle of decline and death in which they are enmeshed.[6]

Time and exemplarity

> 'The reason why time exists is so everything
> doesn't happen at once . . .'
> — Buckaroo Banzai.

Time figures not only in Livy's programmatic statements in the preface but throughout his work.[7] Two aspects are particularly important: first, the historical period that Livy chooses to cover (the form of time, as it were); second, the way in which he uses time and memory within his history (the content of time). Though called *Ab urbe condita*, 'from the founding of the city', his history actually begins some four hundred years earlier, with the fall of Troy: *Iam primum omnium satis constat Troia capta* . . . . (1.1.1 'First of all it is generally agreed that after the capture of Troy . . .'). According to one version, that capture represented the beginning of Rome, and so Livy uses it: the Trojan hero Aeneas arrives in Latium, cements an alliance with the local king, and within three chapters Romulus and Remus, the future founders of Rome, are born (1.4.2).[8] Time telescopes: of the years between the traditional date for the fall of Troy (1184) and that for the founding of Rome (753), the first few are treated at some length (Aeneas and his son Ascanius, together with the two cities they found, Lavinium and Alba Longa, get chapters 1.1–3.5 between them) but all the generations between Ascanius and the twins' grandfather are collapsed into twelve lines of Oxford text (1.3.6–9); Romulus and Remus themselves receive comparatively generous treatment, up through Romulus' death at 1.16. From this point on, time stretches: the history moves forward at an increasingly slow pace, both teasing and gratifying the readers who are 'hurrying ahead': one book for the first 250 years of Rome's existence; four for the next 120; five for the next 97; and so on until, when he reached his own time, Livy was covering only about one year per book.[9]

There is, of course, another way of looking at it. Livy told us in the preface that he enjoys staying away, while he can, from the present, a time in which political cares can disturb – though not compromise – a historian's objectivity (5). Yet time in the past is all too short: though the *Ab urbe condita* illustrates what modern scholars call an 'expansion of the past'[10] and tells in great detail of a long-vanished and undocumented period, Livy's treatment of the early history of Rome is less expansive than some other historians'; as his history continues it becomes ever more detailed, ever more inclusive. The claims of the present are insistent; the closer he comes to his own time, the more he must tell. And it is not certain that he ever finished. The *Ab urbe condita* originally had 142 books, probably published in groups of five ('pentads'), and going up to 9 B.C.[11] We are not sure, however, whether that date was Livy's chosen stopping point (it is not an obvious one, though a case has been made for its appropriateness[12]). Many scholars believe that he originally intended to stop with the death of Cicero in book 120 (43 B.C.), but then changed his mind and continued on through the Augustan period; such an extension is attested for Polybius, for the epic poet Ennius, and for the late-antique historian Ammianus.[13] It is not clear, however, whether Livy himself would have thought of these latter books as an 'addition': his statement, reported by the elder Pliny, that he would have stopped earlier but his 'restless spirit fed on the work', suggests that he would simply have kept on working as long as he could. We will probably never know the truth. It is not implausible, however, that whatever Livy may have intended when he began his history, the end-point of the *Ab urbe condita* was incessantly deferred, as Roman history moved on, and the history of Rome moved with it.[14] History could not come to a full stop, since in a sense the Roman *imperium* defined time, as it defined space: from Livy's perspective, history from the very beginning of the 'historical' period, that is from the Trojan war, was Roman history, as the civilized world was Roman territory.[15]

Time within the *Ab urbe condita* also requires a dual perspective: it is always past (this is history, after all), yet it is also always seen from the present, always filtered through the perspective of the reader. As a popular history of England once put it, 'History is not what you thought. It is *what you can remember*. All other history defeats itself.'[16] But what matters is not only *what* you remember, but how and why. Livy is explicit about what the *memoria rerum gestarum* is for:

ad illa mihi pro se quisque acriter intendat animum, quae uita, qui mores fuerint, per quos uiros quibusque artibus domi militiaeque et partum et auctum imperium sit; labante deinde paulatim disciplina uelut dissidentes primo mores sequatur animo, deinde ut magis magisque lapsi sint, tum ire coeperint praecipites, donec ad haec tempora quibus nec uitia nostra nec remedia pati possumus peruentum est. hoc illud est praecipue in cognitione rerum salubre ac frugiferum, omnis te exempli documenta in illustri posita monumento intueri: inde tibi tuaeque rei publicae quod imitere capias, inde foedum inceptu foedum exitu quod uites.

My concern is that each reader should pay keen attention to these things: what kind of life, what kind of character the Romans had, through what kind of men and by what means power was both acquired and expanded at home and abroad; then, as discipline tottered a little, let him follow that character in his mind as it began to fall apart, so to speak, then as it collapsed more and more, then began to rush headlong, until we have come to these times in which we can endure neither our faults nor their remedies. This in fact is an especially healthy and fruitful element of the study of history, that you contemplate object-lessons of every type of model set up in a perspicuous monument: thence for yourself and your state you can choose what to imitate, thence what to avoid, if it is loathsome in its beginning, loathsome in its outcome.[17]

As we have already seen, Livy thinks of history in general and in particular (that is, his book[18]) as a medicine for the state. In *Praef.* 10 he explains how that medicine is to work. History, he says, is a *monumentum*, a word which can denote either a physical structure or a literary work. It is, crucially, illuminated – *illustre*, 'perspicuous' or 'famous,' means literally 'bright, pervaded with light' (*OLD* 1). History is useful only if it is visible.[19] On the monument, further, are *exempla* – again, a word which can be used of physical copies (*OLD* 9a) but which more often denotes a literary or moral/ethical 'precedent' or 'pattern'.[20] Yet, given the stress in *Praef.* 9 on people (*uita, mores, uiri,* and *artes* all apply to human actors), it is inevitable that we think of this monument as a structure containing or supporting images of people. If the structure is 'well lit,' then these images (statues?) are situated in full public view where they can be carefully inspected (*intueri*).[21] In terms of ancient literary theory, the metaphor implies that Livy's narrative will be clear, immediate, vivid, and make us 'see' the events in our mind's eye; it also implies that we will feel the emotions and understand the thoughts and motives of the actors from inside, as it were.[22] This clarity and immediacy are not simply decorative, however. This monument is there explicitly to be useful, to be 'healthy and fruitful' – and not just for anyone, but for *you*. *Tibi tuaeque rei publicae* is a striking phrase, which suggests that Livy is thinking about his potential reader not simply as an individual, but as a citizen. By looking carefully at the monument (i.e. by reading Livy's history attentively), by understanding its representations (distinguishing good and bad), and then by implementing that understanding, *you* make history work. The *Ab urbe condita* is not the past preserved in amber: it is a record of deeds that you must use, imitating the good and avoiding the bad. In turn, if you get it right, this imitation and avoidance will provide a cure for the current evils of your state. History is effective only when it becomes present.

The process by which the reader comes to learn from and apply the lessons of history is double. In *Praef.* 10 the phrase *omnis exempli documenta*, 'object-lessons of every type of model', is not as tautologous as may at first appear. *Documentum*, which is from the same root as *docere*, means something with which one can teach. An *exemplum*, on the other hand, is something that is or can be copied; in Latin, the word came to mean specifically a famous story or action or character that is held up as a specimen to others.[23] What this sentence suggests, then, is that reader and historian must cooperate: the latter serves as a guide and a teacher, the former not passively absorbing lessons but as an active learner. As the characters in the *Ab urbe condita* work to understand the implications and demands of their own historical situation, so the reader, who is also a citizen in a *res publica*, evaluates, judges, and acts according to the lessons of the past.[24]

Time and memory, then, provide the material from which we can benefit if we read Livy. According to the adage, 'those who do not understand history are doomed to repeat it.' Yet in Livian history it seems that you are precisely encouraged (in the case of good *exempla*) to repeat the past. Such an assumption has led generations of scholars to characterize Livy as one who looks constantly to the 'good old days', wishing for their return, scorning the modern world. The matter is not so simple. As we have seen, though acknowledging the pull of the past, the *Ab urbe condita* moves ahead, eagerly: the past may be pleasurable as a retreat and a source of historical knowledge, but it is only really useful as a tool.[25] Recent studies have emphasized that Livy's *exempla* serve not as immovable precedents but as guides: Livian characters repeatedly deploy old patterns of behaviour in new ways, use traditional arguments to uphold original, innovative proposals, revive ancient practices and restore ancient monuments in order to strengthen the foundations on which the modern state rests. History does repeat itself; but understanding history, in Livy, means being willing to change.[26]

Livy's city

A central aspect of *Praef.* 10 (quoted above), which has come to the fore in recent Livian studies, is the comparison of the *Ab urbe condita* to an architectural structure. In his famous discussion of history in the *De oratore* (above, p. 5), Cicero refers to the *exaedificatio*, or 'building up,' of a work of history; Livy, in writing his narrative, seems to have had the same sort of metaphor in mind. In addition to his highly developed skill at creating and managing literary architectonics (discussed below), Livy, it has been argued, draws upon a specific and particularly Roman model for his literary architecture. Roman literary education was primarily practical and rhetorical, in the sense that it taught students – many of whom would go on to be political orators – to use words as persuasive tools.[27] As such, it devoted a great deal of time to training the mind to assimilate, categorize, and deploy a complex system of conventional motifs and general topics on which one could build a specific argument. These motifs and topics, which range from different types of *captatio benevolentiae* (ways of winning over an audience) to variations on the theme of the 'just' (e.g. 'we should pity suppliants') to means of discrediting an opponent are discussed in ancient rhetorical treatises such as the anonymous early first-century B.C. *Rhetorica ad Herennium*. The rhetorical nature of Roman education and thought was pervasive: though designed primarily for oratory, these topics are found in all types of literature. One of the most widely used means of keeping both general topics and the argument of a specific speech (e.g.) straight in one's memory – indeed, of memorizing any complex system or long list of items – was to assign each one an appropriate image and to arrange them in a mental structure: a house, an arch, a colonnade (*Rhet. Her.* 3.29). Each physical item would then remind the student of the required literary or rhetorical topic. Memory was architectural.[28]

Livy seems to have thought about the 'objects' that made up his history – the events and the actors – in a way similar to that in which Romans thought about memory structures. The images at the beginning of Book 6, for example, are not unlike those of the anonymous author of the *Rhetorica ad Herennium* in his description of how to organize topics: compare Livy's claim to have narrated the deeds of the Romans in five books, 'deeds that are obscured by too much antiquity, like things which are barely visible from a long distance . . . (but now) the deeds that follow will be set out more clearly and more accurately from the second origin of the city . . .' with 'then the backgrounds ought to be neither too bright nor too dim, so that the shadows may not obscure the images nor the lustre make them glitter. . . . the intervals between backgrounds should be of moderate extent . . . for, like the external eye, so the inner eye of thought is less powerful when you have moved the object of sight too near or too far away.'[29] We can imagine the monument in *Praef.* 10 as something like a Roman forum with statues arranged around and in it.[30]

Both the statues and the structure in which they are set are important: both the individual episodes and the narrative as a whole matter. Livy is not alone in making such a close association between *memoria*, history, and physical monuments, though he may be alone in extending it to the form of a written history. But his use of the association is enhanced and facilitated by the Romans' highly developed sense of the traditions attaching to places. In the opening to *De finibus* 5 (chap. 2), Cicero makes Piso explain: 'when looking at (*intuens*) our Senate house . . . I used to think of Scipio, Cato, Laelius, and indeed in particular of my own ancestor; places have such power of recall, that not without reason is the system (*disciplina*) of memory taken from them.' Famous monuments called to mind the stories of famous deeds and famous men;[31] in the same way, as we have seen, from an illuminated *monumentum* comes a *memoria rerum gestarum* that can inspire living men to equal or surpass the glory of past achievements.

Because the *Ab urbe condita* is so big, and because in its original form it covered 750 years of Roman history, it is tempting to think of the text as a written city – one which in some ways has outlasted the physical *Vrbs*.[32] Such a city needs a map; that is, in narrative terms, it needs careful articulation, a structure that allows readers to make sense of where they are and to understand how one part of the city relates to another. Livy's use of narrative structure, together with his placing of significant characters and actions in counterpoise, unifies and strengthens his work, which otherwise would be in danger of collapsing from its own size. Even if one takes into account only the surviving thirty-five books, there is a lot of Livy:[33] if the original 142 books were to have been at all meaningful, they had to be articulated into parts that in turn could be related one to another. The basic chronological organization that all history enjoys – the arrow of time, moving from the past to the present – is not enough to maintain the integrity of such a complex work, in which both sequential and contemporaneous actions are narrated.[34] Livy himself, with his frequent authorial interjections, provides some guidance (see below); in a pioneering study T. J. Luce showed how he also exploits the pentad design in such a way as to shape the story and the reader's experience of that story. Since the publication of Luce's book in 1977, readers have continued to find and illuminate architectonic structures within the *Ab urbe condita*.

So for instance, to take a relatively localized example, Books 5 and 6, the juncture between the first two pentads, are part of at least two competing structures. There is a break here, both in form (between two

published units) and in content: so 5 ends with the Gauls' sack of Rome
and the start of its rebuilding under Camillus' leadership, and 6 begins
with a preface full of images of rebirth.[35] Moving backward from the
end, we find the first half of 5 is occupied with another kind of ending,
the Roman defeat of the Etruscans (5.1–22), concluding one phase of
warfare within Italy. That ending is in turn closely followed by a
beginning: the invasion of the Gauls in mid-book (5.32) gives us a
taste of what is to come in future books when Rome fights the Samnites
(Books 7–11) and Carthage (Books 16–20).[36] The Gauls are both a
danger in themselves and a marker for a new kind of war: in them the
Romans face their first truly foreign enemy, one that will become
paradigmatic for external terror and danger.[37] Book 5, then, in many
ways turns out to be a beginning in which Livy sets the stage, via the
Gauls, for Roman expansion outside of Latium and Etruria. Conversely,
Book 6, apparently a new start, also looks backward: in it Livy is
concerned primarily with internal political struggles of the type that
had preoccupied the Romans since the founding of the republic. In the
Struggle of the Orders the new beginning comes only at the end of 6,
with the opening of the consulate to the plebeians.[38] In addition to
serving as narrative boundaries, however, the two books form a coherent
whole on their own, linked by the person of Camillus, Rome's greatest
general before Scipio Africanus. Appearing first at the opening of 5
(1.2) he leads the Romans against Etruscan Veii and against the Gauls,
then takes part (with mixed success) in both political and military events
throughout 6.[39] In these books, then, we can see Livy playing with the
idea of beginnings and endings via pentad divisions,[40] and superimpos-
ing on that play the smaller, more tightly knit unit of Books 5–6, the life
of Camillus.

A different kind of patterning can be seen in the third decade (Books
21–30), which, though clearly articulated into two pentads, essentially
functions as a single unit telling the single story of the war with
Hannibal.[41] Livy announces it as such: the preface to 21 contains the
conventional claim that the historian's subject is to surpass all others in
greatness, and thereby suggests that these books are marked off as a unit
within a larger whole.[42] The ten books describe a kind of arc, from
Hannibal's invasion of Spain and then of Italy in book 21 via the
disasters at the Ticinus, the Trebia, Lake Trasimene, and Cannae
(21–2), through to the deaths of the Scipiones in Spain (25) and
Hannibal's march on Rome (26), the low point and geographical
centre of the decade. Not all in the first five books is disastrous, however:

Fabius pursues his successful delaying action, while later Marcellus takes Syracuse and wins a battle at Agrigentum, victories bracketing the tragedy in Spain. Moreover, Hannibal's march on Rome is inspired by the certainty that Capua, the Campanian city where he wintered after his first campaign season in Italy, is about to fall to the Romans (26.7). Not only does his attack on Rome come to nothing, but hard on the heels of his retreat Livy narrates the appointment to the Spanish command of P. Cornelius Scipio (26.18–19), the 24-year-old general who will eventually defeat Hannibal himself (30). The major Roman defeats, then, are concentrated in Books 21–2, and the first five books end on a mixed note; but the second five open with apparent disaster avoided, and following that *peripeteia* ('reversal of fortune') they continue toward the final, inevitable Roman supremacy.[43] While there are other theatres of war besides those in which Hannibal himself features, the narrative structure and force of the story rests with the Carthaginian, whose initiative in the first five books is balanced by his retreat in the second, and whose threat is countered by the steady rise of Scipio Africanus, who replaces Fabius Maximus as the charismatic military leader of Rome.

Even this brief sketch shows that one of the large-scale techniques with which Livy links the parts of his history is the repeated returning of the narrative focus to its main actors.[44] The famous character sketch of Hannibal opens the second Punic war (21.1, 4), and Livy returns to evaluate him closer to his defeat (28.12); his opponent Scipio is given several brief but telling appearances (e.g. saving his father's life at 21.46; rallying the survivors of Cannae, 22.53) before his lengthy introduction at 26.18. In addition, he is foreshadowed from the start by the active presence of his father, whose cavalry, even before Hannibal crosses the Alps, meet him in a skirmish that Livy labels as an omen for the war as a whole (21.29). The two generals themselves, however, are kept apart until the very end, where Livy brings them together before Zama: their inequality there, as marked by the difference between their speeches (30.30–1: Hannibal is long-winded and sues for peace, Scipio brief and unrelenting), contrasts with the mutual respect which each first professes for the other (30.30.1). Those speeches, and the reported harangues to their troops which follow (30.32–3), structurally balance the paired exhortations of Scipio's father and Hannibal at 21.40–4 and frame the war narrative as a whole.[45]

The architectural coherence of the third decade (and, *mutatis mutandis*, of the *Ab urbe condita* as a whole) is helped by the fact that

Livy's readers already know the outcome of the war. While on one level such historical knowledge threatens the interest of the narrative – why read it if you know how it comes out? – Livy maintains the tension appropriate to such a story through his narrative immediacy, which as we read enables us to suspend, at least partially, the knowledge that Rome won this (and indeed every other) war. Rome's overall destiny for greatness can be thwarted momentarily on the level of the individual detail: so, for example, the impiety of Flaminius and the consequent disaster at Lake Trasimene could mean the end of the city, and the emotive qualities of the narrative are no less effective for the fact that we know they did not.[46] Yet the historian plays with our awareness, as well, most notably by means of narrative 'seeds' that plant expectations of later events. One such is the cavalry skirmish on the border of Spain (above); another, which also looks ahead to the meeting of Scipio and Hannibal, is the accidental encounter of Scipio and Hasdrubal at the court of the African king Syphax (28.17–18). Similarly, the vignette of the 18–year-old Scipio at the Ticinus not only establishes his courage but also lets Livy announce him as the future Africanus (21.46.8), a cognomen finally granted in the very last sentences of the decade (30.45.6–7).[47] Again, Hannibal's failure to march on Rome after Lake Trasimene, for which he is famously criticized by his lieutenant Maharbal (22.51), foreshadows his later abortive march on the city. In each case, the foreshadowing and the event foreshadowed function reciprocally, their effectiveness in tying the text together depending on the reader's awareness and expectation that something like this will happen again. Each 'seed' thus at the same time both removes suspense and generates it.

A last large-scale device with which Livy ties his history together is his deployment of 'archival' material. Far from being a seamless web (below, p. 97), Livy's narrative can be broadly characterized as a combination of 'episodes' or 'stories'[48] punctuated by two different kinds of non-narrative material, on the one hand, 'scholarly' interventions (reports of variants, citations of sources, cross-references to other parts of the *Ab urbe condita*, etc.), and on the other, reports of state and religious business (appointments or deaths of magistrates and priests, foundations of temples, prodigies and their expiations, famines and pestilences, etc.).[49] This material becomes increasingly more substantial as the text progresses, perhaps because Livy's sources became more detailed, but also perhaps because as the Roman state grew more complex and more organized, such events multiplied. At the beginning of the Republic, the narrative is articulated quite simply from year to year, the archival material often consisting only of the annual elections which are the foundation and sufficient condition for the state's continuing existence.[50] In latei buuks, the years acquire a characteristic 'annalistic' shape, beginning (often) with the elections and reports of prodigies, followed by events abroad (i.e. military campaigns), ending with a return to Rome and more archival material, typically reports of deaths, colonies, etc. J. W. Rich rightly points out that such an organization is often more honoured in the breach than in the observance:[51] one of Livy's most characteristic moves is the modification of conventional narrative expectations, especially on the level of form, and it would be surprising to find him adhering slavishly to a pattern which provided opportunity for play.[52] Since it *is* a pattern, however, and one that Livy's readers come to expect to find, it provides a further kind of 'map' to this written city: as the elections, military assignments, and other such events formed the backbone of the state, so they form the backbone of Livy's narrative, assuring that it, like the state it describes and recreates, moves ahead in predictable, traditional fashion.

A 'tessellation' of styles[53]

It is difficult to generalize about Livy's style. Neither as determinedly outré as Sallust nor as obsessed with the discordant and the bizarre as Tacitus (below, pp.110–11), Livy wrote a Latin whose chief features are a certain supple variety and a love of experimentation. He varies his writing considerably to suit his subject matter, which ranged from wars to weddings to Senate meetings to revolutionary councils; the result was a historiographical style that became the model for later historians such as Curtius Rufus, Velleius Paterculus, and Tacitus.[54] Rather than adding another to the numerous assessments, ancient and modern, of Livy's style, I offer here a close reading of a single passage from the fourth decade, the attack of Antiochus III of Syria on the Thessalian town of Larisa in 192 and his activities in early winter 191:[55]

10. Intra decimum diem quam Pheras uenerat his perfectis, Crannonem profectus cum toto exercitu primo aduentu cepit. ²inde Cierium et Metropolim et iis circumiecta castella recepit; omniaque iam regionis eius praeter Atracem et Gyrtonem in potestate erant. ³tunc adgredi Larisam constituit, ratus uel terrore ceterarum expugnatarum uel beneficio praesidii dimissi uel exemplo tot ciuitatium dedentium sese non ultra in pertinacia mansuros. ⁴elephantis agi ante signa terroris causa iussis, quadrato agmine ad urbem incessit, ut incerti fluctuarentur animi magnae partis Larisaeorum inter metum

praesentem hostium et uerecundiam absentium sociorum. [5]per eosdem dies Amynander cum Athamanum iuuentute occupat Pelinnaeum, et Menippus cum tribus milibus peditum Aetolorum et ducentis equitibus in Perrhaebiam profectus Malloeam et Chyretias ui cepit ⟨et⟩ depopulatus est agrum Tripolitanum. [6]his raptim peractis Larisam ad regem redeunt; consultanti quidnam agendum de Larisa esset superuenerunt. [7]ibi in diuersum sententiae tendebant, aliis uim adhibendam et non differendum censentibus quin operibus ac machinis simul undique moenia adgrederetur urbis sitae in plano, apertae campestri undique aditu, [8]aliis nunc uires urbis nequaquam Pheraeis conferendae memorantibus, nunc hiemem et tempus anni nulli bellicae rei, minime obsidioni atque oppugnationi urbium aptum. [9]incerto regi inter spem metumque legati a Pharsalo qui ad dedendam urbem suam forte uenerant animos auxerunt.

[10]M. Baebius interim cum Philippo in Dassaretiis congressus Ap. Claudium ex communi consilio ad praesidium Larisae misit, qui per Macedoniam magnis itineribus in iugum montium quod super Gonnos est peruenit. [11]oppidum Gonni uiginti milia ab Larisa abest, in ipsis faucibus saltus quae Tempe appellantur situm. [12]ibi castra metatus latius quam pro copiis et plures quam quot satis in usum erant ignes cum accendisset, speciem quam quaesierat hosti fecit, omnem ibi Romanum exercitum cum rege Philippo esse. [13]itaque hiemem instare apud suos causatus rex, unum tantum moratus diem ab Larisa recessit et Demetriadem rediit; Aetolique et Athamanes in suos receperunt se fines. [14]Appius etsi cuius rei causa missus erat solutam cernebat obsidionem, tamen Larisam ad confirmandos in reliquum sociorum animos descendit; [15]duplexque laetitia erat quod et hostes excesserant finibus et intra moenia praesidium Romanum cernebant.

11. Rex Chalcidem a Demetriade profectus, amore captus uirginis Chalcidensis Cleoptolemi filiae, cum patrem primo allegando, deinde coram ipse rogando fatigasset [2]inuitum se grauioris fortunae condicioni illigantem, tandem impetrata re tamquam in media pace nuptias celebrabat et reliquum hiemis, oblitus, quantas simul duas res suscepisset, bellum Romanum et Graeciam liberandam, omissa omnium rerum cura, in conuiuiis et uinum sequentibus uoluptatibus ac deinde ex fatigatione magis quam satietate earum in somno traduxit. [3]eadem omnis praefectos regios, qui ubique, ad Boeotiam maxime, praepositi hibernis erant, cepit luxuria, in eandem et milites effusi sunt; [4]nec quisquam eorum aut arma induit, aut stationem aut uigilias seruauit, aut quicquam quod militaris operis aut muneris esset fecit.

10. These operations were completed within ten days of his reaching Pherae; he then set out to Crannon with his entire army, and took it immediately on arrival. [2]Next he seized Cierium and Metropolis, and the strongholds surrounding them, so that the whole of that region except Atrax and Gyrto was now under his control. [3]He thereupon decided to attack Larisa, thinking that the inhabitants would not remain stubborn any longer, because of the fear inspired by the storming of the other towns, or his kindness in releasing the garrison, or the example of so many states surrendering themselves. [4]He ordered the elephants to be driven before the standards to inspire panic, and advanced on the city in square formation, causing the spirits of a large section of the Larisaeans to waver uncertainly between the immediate fear of the enemy and respect for their absent allies. [5]In the course of these days Amynander with his young Athamanian troops seized Pelinnaeum; and Menippus with 3000 Aetolian infantry and 200 cavalry marched into Perrhaebia, forcibly seized Malloea and Chyretiae, and ravaged the territory of the Tripolis. [6]After speedily accomplishing this, they returned to Larisa to the king, and

came upon him as he sought counsel on what he should do about Larisa. [7]Opinions there varied. Some proposed the use of force, and no postponement of a simultaneous attack from all sides with siege-works and engines against the walls of a city set on level ground, exposed on all sides over the level plain; [8]others argued now that the city's strength was in no way comparable to that of the Pheraeans, now that winter and the time of the year were suited to no war-operations, least of all to blockading and attacking cities. [9]As the king wavered between hope and fear, the chance arrival of ambassadors from Pharsalus who had come to surrender their city raised his spirits.

[10]In the meantime Marcus Baebius had joined with Philip in the territory of the Dassaretii, and following their joint consultation sent Appius Claudius to defend Larisa. By forced marches through Macedonia he reached the mountain-ridge above Gonni, [11]a town twenty miles from Larisa situated in the very jaws of the gorge called Tempe. [12]There he measured out a camp larger than his forces required, and lit more fires than were enough for their needs, thus giving the enemy the desired impression that the whole Roman army was there and King Philip as well. [13]So Antiochus after only a day's delay retreated from Larisa and returned to Demetrias, with the excuse to his forces that winter was upon them. The Aetolians and Athamanians retired to their own territories. [14]Though Appius realized that the siege had been raised and the purpose of his journey fulfilled, he nonetheless went down to Larisa to strengthen the resolve of the allies for the future. [15]There was twofold joy, both because the enemy had quitted their territory and because they saw a Roman garrison between their walls.

11. The king set out from Demetrias to Chalcis. There he was smitten with love for a maiden of Chalcis, the daughter of Cleoptolemus. At first by messengers and then by face-to-face requests he wearied the father, [2]who was reluctant to involve himself in a relationship which threatened a more oppressive future. But finally the king obtained his request and continued to celebrate the marriage as though in an era of peace. He dismissed from his mind the two great burdens which he had simultaneously undertaken, war with Rome and the liberation of Greece; and abandoning responsibility for all affairs, he spent the rest of the winter in feasting, in the pleasures which attend on wine, and then in the sleep which followed exhaustion rather than repletion. [3]The same degenerate living dominated the king's lieutenants who commanded in winter-quarters everywhere, especially in Boeotia, and the soldiers eagerly followed suit. [4]None of them either wore armour or manned guard-posts and maintained patrols, or performed any military tasks or duties.[56]

This extract falls into two parts: Antiochus' attack on Larisa together with the Roman response, followed by the king's retreat and his marriage. On the one hand, the parts have distinct and contrasting settings, the one a self-contained story of a military action, the other a brief, equally self-contained anecdote about a king's leisure. On the other, the military narrative is not definitively separated from the following domestic scene. The information that the campaign season was ending is provided obliquely in two reported remarks (10.8 *hiemem*, 10.13 *hiemem instare*). So unobtrusive a transition from campaign to winter quarters is not unparalleled in Livy, but he more often chooses to delineate the stages of an action, or the shift from one action to another, explicitly: in this extract an example is 10.1, *intra decimum diem . . . . perfectis* (cf. also 10.5 *per eosdem dies* and 10.10 *interim*).[57] We are therefore encouraged to read the military and domestic parts of this extract as forming some sort of unity.

What ties them together is the character of Antiochus himself. We first see him taking Crannon by storm immediately upon arriving (*primo aduentu*), then several other towns in quick succession (10.1–2): such rapid conquest is one of the conventional marks of an ideal general,[58] and identifies the king as a force to be reckoned with. As he approaches Larisa, his motivation for attacking it is detailed by Livy in what is called a '*ratus*-period', a clause governed by the participle *ratus*, 'thinking that', a common device for getting inside a character's head (10.3). Antiochus' shrewd surmise about why the Larisaeans might surrender revolves around the notions of mutual favour – he has done them a *beneficium*, a kindness, which they will feel bound to return – and precedent – they will deduce from what happened to the towns already captured by Antiochus that resistance is futile, or they will copy the example of the people around them who are surrendering: i.e. they will either avoid or imitate the *exempla* available to them. In counting on Larisa's looking to the fate of its neighbours, Livy's Antiochus may be 'imitating' the later Julius Caesar, the greatest general of them all, who at *Bellum ciuile* 3.80–1 relates how several towns in this same part of Thessaly surrendered to him after he sacked one that resisted. The echo is playful: the one town that did *not* surrender, Caesar tells us, was Larisa (*BC* 3.81.2).[59]

Larisa wavers (10.4 *incerti . . . inter metum . . . . et uerecundiam*). At this moment, however, Livy shifts the narrative to another part of Greece, reporting on the contemporaneous victories of Antiochus' lieutenants. Timed to coincide with the deliberations of the towns-people, the narrative break opens up a hole in the Syrian king's apparently successful enterprise. Though the focus returns to Larisa along with Amynander and Menippus,[60] Antiochus has lost narrative control: he is now object, not subject (10.6 *ad regem redeunt*), and – in a couple of awkward sentences perhaps mirroring the jolt we feel as readers – his subordinates find the king himself trying to decide what to do. His indecision is communicated to his advisers: some counsel one thing, others another, as the sentence opens up into a long appended ablative absolute further subdivided into parts (10.7–8). At the end of the council, far from having resolved the issue, the king, like the

Larisaeans, and in similar words, wavers (10.9 *incerto . . . inter spem metumque*).

Again, however, the situation alters. In the midst of Antiochus' doubt comes the report of Pharsalus' surrender, brought by legates who arrive *forte*, 'by chance' (10.9).[61] *Forte* often serves to mark a convenient 'coincidence' that in turn triggers a decisive event: for example, Brutus returns *forte* to Rome at the same moment as Lucretia's husband and father go to answer her distress call (1.58.6) – and it is Brutus, of course, who as a result of her rape will take the initiative in expelling the kings from Rome. *Forte* is a narrative clue that suggests significant action. Here, however, the king's new courage is immediately thwarted, as Livy breaks off the narrative a second time. The scene to which he switches with *interim* (10.10) involves not the king's allies but the Romans, who come to Larisa's rescue. Despite the fact that *not* to be fooled is an essential characteristic of the ideal general, Appius' fairly conventional ruse with the campfires deceives Antiochus, who then retreats.[62] Both the enemy's departure and the enclosing within the walls of the Roman *praesidium* are closural gestures, the former putting an end to the siege, the latter a literal rounding off.[63] And by the time we come to that rounding off, the narrative focus has shifted entirely. The attack – unusually for Livy, who likes to show the reactions of those *inside* a besieged town – was with one exception told from the point of view of the aggressors;[64] at the end, however, events are focalized by the townspeople.[65] In a sense, then, Antiochus has lost a textual battle as well as having to abandon a real one.[66]

The episode's coda, the account of the king's marriage at Chalcis,[67] reprises its main themes. Antiochus appears here in the same light as he did in the battle narrative: he leaves one town and approaches another (11.1 *Chalcidem a Demetriade profectus*); is seized by desire (*captus amore*) and makes a finely judged attack (*primo allegando, deinde . . . rogando*) on a wavering enemy (11.2 *inuitum*). This time he is successful (*impetrata re*). That success, however, is no better managed than his siege of Larisa: though he takes the initiative, he is in fact not in charge, but is 'captured' from the start. He spends the winter as if in peacetime, forgetful of his business as king, and his entire army, commander and soldier alike, does the same.[68] This display of bad judgment reflects and helps explain Antiochus' previous military failure, albeit in abbreviated form (the attack, which will have lasted a relatively short time, takes nearly four times as long to relate as does the winter). Livy's compression produces at least one remarkable effect: the description of the king's activities (11.2 *reliquum hiemis . . . in somno traduxit*) must indicate repeated feasting, pleasures, etc. (presumably interspersed with other activities) over the course of several months, but the only possible hint of this duration of time is the imperfect *celebrabat* ('continued to cele-brate').[69] But Latin regularly uses the imperfect for subordinate actions and the aoristic perfect (here *traduxit*) for the primary action; in this sentence, then, the imperfect may have little continuative force, and the last words, *in somno traduxit*, give the impression that Antiochus passed his winter all at once in a drunken, sated sleep. For the experienced reader of history, the closing detail that Antiochus indulged in his pleasures to exhaustion rather than repletion identifies him as the opposite of a good general, since the latter takes only what he needs and no more.[70] Our final glimpse of him, then, is as someone precisely opposite to the man implied by his vigorous entrance at 10.1.

So far, this close reading shows us a deceptively simple narrative in which we are led to form an opinion about Antiochus that conflicts with our first impression of him as a decisive, praiseworthy commander. To see how the Latin itself works, however, we have to look more closely. In discussing style, scholars generally consider four areas: diction (the words used, especially with regard to how 'choice' – i.e. archaic, innovative, or otherwise unusual – they are),[71] syntax (the arrangement of the words into clauses, the 'grammar'), sentence structure (long or short? simple or complex?), and figures (special ways of using language, either to produce artistic sounds – e.g. with rhyme – or 'poetic' effects through tropes such as simile or metaphor). Ancient writers thought carefully about these while composing,[72] as the choices they made in each area would determine what sort of literary work they produced.[73]

Historians of Rome had to narrate a great many battles. A conventional vocabulary, which is on display most clearly in the Caesarian *commentarii*, gradually grew up for such descriptions.[74] Livy's narratives of military action borrow techniques from Caesar, often imitating what has been called 'communiqué style' (the terse, telegraphic language in which dispatches from a legate to his commander or to the Senate might have been couched).[75] Other conventional elements include the capture *primo aduentu* (10.1, see above); the advance in square formation (10.4 *quadrato agmine*) and the forced march (10.10 *magnis itineribus*), all found frequently in any war narrative. Similarly, the almost formulaic language used to effect a transition from one part of the story to the next – *his perfectis, profectus* + accusative of end of motion, *per eosdem dies, his raptim peractis, interim* – is abundant in (though not exclusive to) military narrative.[76] This style, however, is mixed with language that looks conventional but which in fact seems to be made up of Livy's own invented military 'clichés.' So, for instance, *propositum signum* ('the setting up of a signal'), *motum certamen* ('the fight that has been set in motion'), and *proelium omittere* ('to abandon a battle'), all of which are found either first or exclusively in Livy, occur inside a couple of pages at 6.12–13. The effect is one of slightly unbalanced familiarity: this is military language, but not as we know it. 'Military' expressions in our extract include the jingle *obsidioni atque oppugnationi* (10.8; otherwise the combination of nouns is found only in Caesar). If the speaker intends them as near-synonyms, as they often appear to be,[77] then this is an illustration of 'fullness of expression' (*copia uerborum*) sometimes affected by Livy: cf. also the tautologous *hiemem et tempus anni* (10.8) and *operibus ac machinis* (10.7). This last is also, apparently, a Livian expression: both *opera* and *machinae* (or *machinationes, machinamenta*) designate siege-works (the former a general, the latter a specific type); outside Livy their combination is found only in the Flavian writer Frontinus (*Strat.* 3 *Praef.*) and (slightly modified) at Tac. *H.* 4.28.3 (*machinas molemque operum*).

Apart from these military expressions, the diction in this extract has a perhaps surprising number of choice elements for such a short, not obviously 'written-up' passage. Unusual language includes the emotive combination of *incertus* and *fluctuari* (10.4),[78] *superuenire* (10.6, first at Verg. *E.* 6.20 and perhaps coined by the poet; otherwise primarily in Livy before the imperial period[79]); 10.7 *non differendum quin* (first and almost exclusively in Livy[80]); *fauces saltus* (10.11, perhaps borrowed from the republican tragedian Accius, whose fragments have the only extant example before Livy[81]); *amore captus* (11.1, poetic[82]); *celebrare* of a wedding (11.2, first in prose in Livy[83]); *effusi in luxuriam* (11.3, the 'middle' voice of *effundere* in this sense is first in Livy[84]). There is a particularly striking use of the preposition *ad* to mean 'in' (11.3), which may be colloquial and which seems almost confined to Livy in literary Latin.[85]

The rich texture imparted by this vocabulary is further enhanced by *variatio*, or deliberate variation, and consequent play with the reader's expectations. This is a technique associated above all with Tacitus (below, pp. 110–11); Livy uses it subtly, producing a slight imbalance in his prose that makes the reader work.[86] Four examples stand out in this extract: the frustrated parallelism in *inter metum praesentem hostium et uerecundiam absentium sociorum* (10.4), where by transferring the epithet *praesens* from the enemy to the fear Livy upsets the otherwise exact correspondence between the two halves of the prepositional phrase; the varied construction of the modifiers of *urbis* at 10.7 (adjective + adjective + ablative of description); the extremely unusual joining by *et* of a participle to a *cum*-clause (10. 12 *metatus . . . et cum accendisset*);[87] and the use of *cernere* in two different senses within the same sentence (10.14–15 *cernebat* 'realized'; *cernebant* '(physically) saw'[88]).

In his 'structural artistry' – syntax and arrangement – Livy again demonstrates a varied technique.[89] Much of the scene at Larisa is told simply, with little complex subordination; the sentence in which Antiochus' lieutenants come upon him is particularly remarkable for its repetition of the town's name (10.6), a repetition perhaps caused by Livy's use of parataxis (avoidance of hierarchical syntax).[90] There is plenty of decoration, however, in word order, including several *tricola* (groups of three items, often – but not always – of increasing length), at 10.3 (*uel terrore . . . uel beneficio . . . uel exemplo*[91]), 10.7 (*sitae . . . aditu*, in which the central item, *apertae*, is significantly shorter than the others), and 11.2 (*in conuiuiis . . . earum*). Groups of two elements are also found, notably at 10.8 (*nunc . . . nunc*[92]), 10.12 (*latius quam pro . . . plures quam quot*), and 11.1 (*primo . . . deinde*), where the structure is emphasized by the rhyme, or homoioteleuton, of *allegando . . . rogando*.[93] Hyperbaton, the artistic dislocation of expected word order, is found twice, once at 10.3, where the resulting word order mirrors the enemy retreat within their territory (*in suos se receperunt fines*); and once at 11.3, where *luxuria* is postponed from its natural position next to *eadem* to the end of its clause, to allow it to interact also with *in eandem*.[94]

Writing history is a complicated business, not least because according to the canons of ancient historiography one was expected to make one's characters speak as well as act. Livy, who was famous in antiquity for his speeches (Quint. 10.1.101, Suet. *Dom.* 10.3), used both reported speech (*oratio obliqua*) and direct discourse (*oratio recta*) throughout his work.[95] Though we will not be looking at any direct speech, there is reported speech in this extract, notably in the deliberations of Antiochus and his lieutenants (10.7–8). This short section illustrates the kind of period (=sentence) that Livy tends to write in imitation of 'real' speech, that is, the kind of speech that one might hear from an orator or in a senate session. Its structure is quite rangy, beginning with a simple main clause as a heading ('opinions varied'), then branching off into parallel ablatives absolute (*aliis . . . censentibus . . . aliis . . .*

memorantibus) reporting the advice given by the different groups. The second clause is longer, and subdivided into two (*nunc . . . nunc*); each ablative absolute has an extension following its 'main' verb (the present participle). While the sentence gives us a lot of information, it describes rather than narrates: nothing actually happens aside from our 'hearing' the words of the king's advisers.

The situation is quite different at 11.1–2.[96] This period, also hypotactic (that is, characterized by subordination rather than coordination), is otherwise radically different from the one just analysed. Here, Livy narrates a sequence of actions, from Antiochus' leaving Demetrias to his arrival at Chalcis, his falling in love, wooing, and wedding, and his behaviour during the winter. It is a typical historiographical period, in which each verbal unit (participle, *cum*-clause, ablative absolute, indicative verb) represents a different stage in the action (the forward-moving narrative units are *profectus . . . captus . . . fatigasset . . . . impetrata . . . . celebrabat . . . . oblitus . . . . traduxit*). There is grammatical subordination but no real subordination of thought.[97] With its two indicative verbs the sentence further illustrates one of the two chief types of narrative period, the so-called '*phrase à relance*,' in which one sequence of subordinate clauses + indicative verb is followed by a second, joined to the first by 'and' or 'but,' as if the sentence had started again.[98] Livy tends to pack his narrative periods full. In this one, the skeleton of forward-moving units is elaborated by other verbs which instead of moving the story ahead function descriptively: the pair of gerunds detailing how Antiochus wore the father down; *illigantem*, of the action the father resists; *omissa*, expanding *oblitus*; and the *tricolon* of activities in which the king spends the winter.[99]

'Livy'

A recent discussion of Livy stresses his openness: 'what makes Livy an Augustan author . . . is not a fixed ideology, but his constant formulation and reformulation of some of the central ideas of his age', among which are reckoned a concern with moral decay and the need for regeneration; patriotism; the value of the past for transforming the present; and the 'realization that . . . . permanence incorporates evolution and change'.[100] Many of these are ideas on which this chapter has also touched. Our reading of the Antiochus episode allows us to go further. Livy took seriously the ancient notion that language mirrors reality. The world of Rome as Livy builds it sometimes looks simple, old-fashioned, full of good old Romans doing good old Roman things: but to take it that way is a mistake. At a fundamental level the present and the past are inextricably entwined, both linguistically (archaisms and neologisms appear in the same sentence; 'real' clichés and invented ones combine in a single description) and thematically. This variety, which is also very Augustan, does more than sustain 'the breadth and movement of the work'.[101] Like the styles of Sallust and of Tacitus, it reflects the world as Livy saw it and as he wants *you* to see it.

It is often pointed out, for example, that Livy's ancient Rome, even as far back as the monarchic period, is working through the same kinds of political and social issues as the late republican and early Augustan periods.[102] Though well aware of historical change,[103] Livy uses this overlay of historical periods to suggest ways in which through close observation of past events we can find ways of approaching present problems. We see both what ancient Rome was like and what implications problems and challenges like our own may have for the construction of our character and our identity. There is a complex layering of audiences in the *Ab urbe condita*: we read/watch the events, but within the text as well people observe the deeds both of their contemporaries (1.24–5, the Romans and Albans watch the battle between the Horatii and Curiatii; 6.20, the *plebs* watch the trial of Manlius Capitolinus; 21.42, Hannibal's soldiers watch the prize fight he stages before the battle at the Ticinus) and of their own ancestors, as related to them in stories and *exempla* and symbolized by monuments.[104] At each level, we and they are invited to see exactly how the past can be useful, and how the present can be negotiated.

This world in which the expected and the paradoxical combine is one in which conventional sources and forms of authority cannot always be taken for granted. The republic that Livy shows us in the surviving books, with its predictable annual rotations and its expanding power, is shadowed always by the knowledge given to us in the Preface, that this monumental Rome is collapsing – has indeed already collapsed (*Praef.* 9). And as if to keep this here-and-now firmly in our mind, Livy makes Augustus, the man who perhaps most of all represents the present, appear already – though only briefly – in the very early books. First mentioned as a peace-keeper who has shut the doors of the temple of Janus (1.19.3), he appears a second time at 4.20.7, as both an innovator and a follower of tradition, 'the founder and restorer of all temples.'[105] In Book 4, however, Livy is primarily interested in Augustus as a source of historical information, reporting the *princeps*' discovery of evidence proving that A. Cornelius Cossus was consul when he dedicated the *spolia opima* ('choice' or 'rich spoils') in 437 B.C.[106] But the way in which he introduces the *princeps*' testimony into his narrative is disconcerting to say the least. Livy first appears to accept Augustus' report (4.20.7), then to cast doubt on it (§§8–10), then to deny that any certainty is possible (§11a) – and finally to return to trusting the inscription Augustus claimed to discover (§11b). When this passage is read in the larger context of the surrounding narrative, however, it seems that Livy does in fact reject Augustus' information (4.32.4). 'Thus the author has succeeded in acknowledging Augustus' personal authority generously and uncompromisingly while at the same time undermining it.'[107] Part of what is going on here is Livy's assertion of his own competence as a historian: Augustus may have been ruler, but Livy was the scholar.[108] The context of the discussion, however, is important. The *spolia opima* comprised the armour of an enemy leader killed by a Roman general who was endowed with *imperium* and who had been fighting under his own auspices. At the time of writing, the rank of the previous dedicators was of immediate political relevance, as Augustus had just blocked M. Licinius Crassus' claim to have the right to make a similar dedication, basing his refusal on the fact that Crassus was not fighting under his own auspices and did not have the same status as his three predecessors. It is therefore inescapable that in citing Augustus only to disagree with him (however generously) Livy is declaring his independence from the wider political authority that the *princeps* could potentially – and on rare occasions, later, would actually – wield, even in the sphere of literature.[109] Though the emperor and the historian seem to have shared many elements of a moral and social programme, Livy was fundamentally detached from politics.[110] Detached but not dispassionate: Livy's concern with moral regeneration involves him in investigation and criticism of aristocrats and plebeians, of Rome's behaviour toward foreigners and of their problematic influence on Rome, of leaders and led alike.[111]

If that is the case, then we need to ask what kind of authority Livy claims. We know very little about the real Livy;[112] but who is the author who is implied in the pages of the *Ab urbe condita*?[113] His most striking characteristic, evident from the very first words of the Preface and displayed throughout the text thereafter, is a kind of arrogant deference. The first thing we hear is his wondering if his project will be worthwhile; yet that project is one that would take him a lifetime and 142 books, history on a scale never yet achieved in either Greek or Latin.[114] He says he will console himself if his name is obscured by the nobility of those who will put him in the shade (*Praef.* 3); yet there is a remarkable accumulation of first-person verbs in the Preface, and his history as a whole opens with the foundation *first* of Padua, Livy's birthplace, and only secondly of the settlement in Latium that would eventually lead to Rome (1.1.2–3).[115]

As we read through the text, we meet 'Livy' frequently. He keeps us on our moral and ethical toes: invites us to read an episode in a particular way (e.g. 6.22.6); praises or blames the people whose deeds he records (22.3 Flaminius; 28.12, Hannibal); uses speeches to open debate on important political and social issues (4.3–5, 34.1–8). He helps us read history: tells us whether a story is plausible or not (5.21.8–9); alerts us to conflicts among his sources over a name (1.3.3), a number (26.49.6), a date (2.21.3), or the way something happened (39.43.4); explains that some kinds of evidence are by nature unreliable (8.40.4, 38.56.5); insists that one of a historian's duties is to report tradition, whether believable or not (8.18.2–3).[116] Finally, he pushes us to use the monument, guiding us physically and intellectually through this city, pointing out where contemporary Rome bears traces of ancient Rome, in an inscription (6.4.3) or a significant place (5.50.5), and showing us where and how an older custom or belief is different from today's (43.13.1–2).[117]

More challenging still, Livy invites his readers to participate in evaluating the past by confronting us repeatedly with situations that are difficult, sometimes impossible, to resolve or to judge. In the words of one recent critic, 'the narrator's own uncertainty, confusion, and conspicuous arbitrariness serve to dramatize the logic of his argument, that a confident determination of historical fact is beyond reach.'[118] What he substitutes for such confidence is the repeated demand that we examine and test our assumptions about Roman identity as constructed by Roman tradition. As a professional scholar, a non-participant in the political and military world he describes, Livy risked and still risks having his authority questioned, even dismissed.[119] It is possible, however, to read his 'deferential' approach, his professions of insecurity and doubt, both as guarantees of his reliability (analogous in some ways to modern footnotes) and as a pose that enables him to question, even partially to subvert, the Rome he is trying to mend.[120]

Subversion, however, is only part of the picture. As C. B. R. Pelling has recently stressed, critics tend to look only for ways in which a text challenges its readers' beliefs and assumptions.[121] There are other possible models, however. Building on general studies of the meaning and nature of propaganda, A. Wallace-Hadrill and others have shown that one of the principal (and perhaps unconscious) concerns of Augustan writers was to make sense of Augustus and his new world by inscribing them into the values and traditions with which those writers were familiar.[122] In some ways this was very difficult, since Augustus represented a break with the past. But a continual testing of the possibility and success of contemporary experiments in art, in politics, and in social reform does not necessarily mean a rejection of those experiments.[123] Augustus worked, and succeeded, by a process of trial and error; he succeeded as well by blending innovation with tradition, presenting new, often radical ideas as incarnations of the old.[124] We have seen that Livy similarly mixes the old with the new, producing a history that has an unmistakable 'thematic and ideological coherence.'[125] The *Ab urbe condita* is at once a criticism and a celebration of Rome, a text which both affirms and questions the traditions on which the city was built, and with which it may rebuild itself.

NOTES

1. *OLD memoria* 7, 8; see above, p. 1.

2. Seneca (*Ep.* 100.9) says that Livy wrote dialogues that were 'partway between history and philosophy'; scholars have tended to accept this testimony (so Ogilvie (²1970), 2, Walsh (1961), 4, 205) though no trace of these works has survived. He also is said to have written a 'letter' to his son giving advice on reading matter for the would-be orator (Quint. 10.1.39). Livy must have composed the *Ab urbe condita* at the rate (on average) of three books per year, starting some time in the mid-30s B.C. (he was born ca. 64), and continuing on till his death ca. A.D. 17. For the evidence and discussion of these dates see Luce (1965), 231 with n. 61.

3. Note also Moles (1993), 146 on *pro uirili parte*: 'Livy's historical project is itself exemplary of 'virile' individual public service'; on Livy's borrowings from and challenges to Sallust in the preface see Moles (1993), 155–62 with further references; on Sallust's history as politics see above, pp. 13–14.

4. On *festinantibus* see Moles (1993), 146–7: 'Livy's readers are readers "in a hurry", hence the size of the *res* [Livy's task] poses difficulties for readers as well as historian . . . the *festinantes* [have] an unhealthy preoccupation with the present or recent past . . . Livy will advocate . . . critical and slow reading commensurate with the size of his subject-matter – the past from the very beginning all the way down to the present.' More on Livy's *persona* above, pp. 70–4.

5. The motif is illustrated at *RICH*, 133–4; see also Moles (1993), 151–2 on the *remedia*.

6. *Praef.* 12, the Romans are 'in love with death both individual and collective', de Selincourt's translation of *desiderium . . . pereundi perdendique omnia*.

7. On time in historiography see A. Momigliano, *Essays in Ancient and Modern Historiography* (1977), 179–204 and Woodman–Martin (1996), 407; on time in Livy see Chaplin (1993) and Miles (1995), 75–109 (orig. published 1986).

8. On the Trojan legend and Rome see now Cornell (1995), 63–8.

9. The pace is not uniform; for a detailed chart see Stadter (1972), 304–7.

10. The expression is that of Badian (1966), 11–13.

11. This statement requires some qualification. The last 22 books (121–42), seem not to have

been organized in the same way as 1–120 (Stadter (1972), 300), while the general scheme of publication in pentads is questioned by some (e.g. D. S. Levene, review of Kraus (1994), *CR* 46 (1996), 50). Book 1 may have been separately published (see Luce (1965), 210 n. 2); and many accept the persuasive hypothesis that the first pentad was reissued in a second edition between 27 and 25 B.C. (below, n. 106). We have very broad outlines of the contents of the missing books (with the exception of Books 136–7) in late-antique summaries, or *periochae*; on them see C. M. Begbie, 'The epitome of Livy', *CQ* 17 (1967), 332–8. The history was transmitted in a manuscript tradition of groups of ten books ('decades').

12. *RICH*, 139 (following Syme).

13. For discussion of the 'appendix' and further references see Kraus (1994), 7–8. Diodorus Siculus (above, p. 8 n. 7) curtailed his original plan, ending with 60 rather than 46 B.C.

14. See especially J. Henderson, 'Livy and the invention of history', in A. Cameron, ed., *History as Text* (London, 1989), 66–85.

15. On Homer as history see *RICH*, 1 with nn. 1–5 and above, p. 48 n. 108; whether or not the ancients drew a definitive line (as Fornara (1983), 4–10 argues) between legendary and historical time, they do speak of a natural boundary at least partly imposed by literary preservation: cf. Horace's 'there lived many great men before Agamemnon' (but without Homer to write about them, they have effectively never existed: *Odes* 4.9.25–6). The equation of the city (*urbs*) with the world (*orbis*) is an Augustan concept with roots in late-republican thought: see now F. Muecke, 'Horace's Rome', *Classicum* 21 (1995), 29–35.

16. W. C. Sellar and R. J. Yeatman, *1066 and All That* (London, 1930), v. On the two temporal perspectives in Livy see further Jaeger (1997).

17. For elements of the translation I draw on the version at *RICH*, 130.

18. Moles (1993), 153.

19. So for example when at 6.1.2 Livy complains that the events he has just narrated in Books 1–5 were hard to see, we should think back to this sentence; his promise to go on and make things *clariora*, 'more famous' or 'brighter,' is a promise to make subsequent history easier for us to see (on the dual application of *clarus* to literary and physical visibility see *OLD* 2, 6, 8).

20. On *exemplum* in Livy see Chaplin (1993), 11–18.

21. On *intueri* see Kraus (1994), 171, Moles (1993), 166 nn. 61–3. On the importance for Livy of character see below, n. 44.

22. The technical terms for this literary clarity are *enargeia* ('graphic presentation') or *euidentia*: there is a good discussion at Walsh (1961), 181–90; see also *RICH*, 233 s.v. 'vivid description' (Index) and Vasaly (1993), 20 n. 6. On the audience feeling emotions see M. Winterbottom, 'On impulse', in Innes–Hine–Pelling (1995), 315.

23. On *documentum*, which 'always has a didactic component', see Chaplin (1993), 17; on exemplarity see further S. Goldhill, 'The failure of exemplarity' in de Jong–Sullivan (1994). For more on the Roman preoccupation with images of the past see M. Bettini, '"The future at your back": spatial representations of time in Latin' in *Anthropology and Roman Culture* (Baltimore, 1991), 113–93.

24. The narrator's frequent interventions help this process (above, p. 73). The role of the reader and Livy's text has received much attention recently; see e.g. Levene (1993), 29–30, Moles (1993), *passim*, Miles (1995), 8–74.

25. On the combination of pleasure (*dulce*) and usefulness (*utile*) in the Preface see Moles (1993), 141–2.

26. Chaplin (1993), 125–54; Miles (1995), 249 s.v. 'T. Livius and: historical change and continuity' (Index); on repetition in Livy see further C. S. Kraus, 'Repetition and empire in the *Ab urbe condita*', forthcoming in a collection edd. C. Foss and P. E. Knox (Stuttgart).

27. On ancient education see S. F. Bonner, *Education in Ancient Rome* (Berkeley, 1977); the primary ancient text is Quintilian, *Institutio Oratoria*.

28. Kraus (1994a), 268 with the references in n. 6; see also Vasaly (1993), 1–5 and the Introduction to Jaeger (1997).

29. 6.1.2, 3 *res cum uetustate nimia obscuras uelut quae magno ex interuallo loci uix cernuntur . . . clariora deinceps certioraque ab secunda origine . . . . urbis gesta . . . exponentur; Rhet. Her.* 3.32 *tum nec nimis illustres* [cf. *Praef.* 10] *nec uehementer obscuros locos habere oportet, ne aut obcaecentur tenebris imagines aut splendore praefulgent. interualla locorum mediocria placet esse . . . nam ut aspectus item cogitatio minus ualet siue nimis procul remoueris siue uehementer prope admoueris id*

quod oportet uideri. On space, topography, and memory see further M. K. Jaeger, *'Custodia fidelis memoriae:* Livy's story of M. Manlius Capitolinus', *Latomus* 52 (1993), 350–63.

30. The monument to which it is most commonly compared is the Forum of Augustus, though that was not built until the end of the century: T. J. Luce, 'Livy, Augustus, and the Forum Augustum', in Raaflaub–Toher (1990), 123–38.

31. Vasaly (1993), 26–39; cf. also Sall. *BJ* 4.5, quoted above, p. 10 (portraits have the same inspirational value).

32. So e.g. M. Serres, *Livy: the Book of Foundations* (Berkeley, 1991), 140; for a detailed study of this aspect of Livy see Jaeger (1997).

33. So the poet Martial (first century A.D.) claims that his library cannot hold all of 'huge [*ingens*] Livy' (14.190).

34. Cf. the chronological difficulties that arise when Livy describes different theatres of activity (Greece, Italy, etc.) as the empire expanded: on these, and on Livy's method of coping with them, see Luce (1977), 33–138.

35. The second pentad has been analysed by J. Lipovsky, *A Historiographical Study of Livy Books VI–X* (Salem, N. H. 1981).

36. Books 6–15 formed one division of the history (Stadter (1972), 293–4); but though the last Samnite war continued into book 11, Livy did in some ways also articulate 6–10 as a self-contained unit: for argument see Oakley (1997), 112–14.

37. So Sall. *BJ* 114.2 (quoted above, p. 26) with Paul (1984), 257: 'fear of the Gauls was traditional at Rome.'

38. On that event, still the subject of much debate among historians, see Oakley (1997) on 6.34.

39. On Camillus see Ogilvie (²1970), 631, 741–3, E. Burck, 'Die Gestalt des Camillus,' in *Wege zu Livius*, ed. E. Burck (Darmstadt, 1967), 310–28, and Miles (1995), 110–36 (orig. published 1988). Camillus dies just inside Book 7 (1.8–10), which therefore also looks back, just as the close of 6 looks ahead (the full results of the elections held at 6.42.9 are not announced until 7.1.2). For the many responsions between Books 5 and 6 see Kraus (1994), 348 s.v. 'Livy: *Ab urbe condita* 6: ~ Book 5' (Index).

40. And perhaps playing with earlier texts: Claudius Quadrigarius *began* with the sack of Rome, where Livy *ends* a unit. See also below, pp. 88–97.

41. 21–30 may have been unique in their decade pattern (Oakley (1997), 111); see also Luce (1977), 27–8. The fundamental study of these books is E. Burck, *Einführung in die dritte Dekade des Livius* (Heidelberg, ²1962); see also his article, 'The third decade' in T. A. Dorey, ed., *Livy* (London, 1971), 21–46 and Levene (1993), 38–77.

42. 'Most historians have prefaced their work by stressing the importance of the period they propose to deal with; and I may well, at this point, follow their example and declare that I am now about to tell the story of the most memorable war in history' (21.1.1); the first unambiguous example is Thucydides 1.1.1, which Livy echoes here (see P. G. Walsh, ed., *Livy: Book 21* (repr. Bristol, 1991), 121). Some of the later books may similarly have been organized by war, though the wars do not correspond to textual decades; so e.g. the *periochae* for 109–116 are 'subtitled' *qui est ciuilis belli primus* ('being the first book of the civil war') etc., perhaps reflecting a pattern perceived by Livian readers: see Stadter (1972), 297–8.

43. *Peripeteia* is a term borrowed from criticism of drama and frequently used to indicate the turning points, both large and small, in Livy's narrative; see Walsh (1961), 202, 210, 213 and (more generally) Chausserie-Laprée (1969), 541–648 on 'Les techniques de rupture.'

44. For Livy's concentration on people see e.g. R. M. Ogilvie in *CHCL* 2.459–60: 'he saw history in terms of human personalities and representative individuals . . . for Livy, human nature . . . determines the course of human events.' There is extended, though now somewhat dated, discussion of the moral aspects of Livy's characterization at Walsh (1961), 82–109. Preoccupation with human actors is found throughout Roman historiography (for Sallust see above, pp. 32–9), as well as in the idea, explicit in Cicero and Livy, that the eternal body of the state consists of the unending series of the mortal bodies and deeds of great men (Kraus (1994), 16–17 with n. 69).

45. These are the only examples of paired exhortations in Livy (Luce (1977), 27 n. 58); on the genre of pre-battle *hortationes* see the articles listed at Woodman-Martin (1996), 346, adding C. T. H. R. Ehrhardt, 'Speeches before battle?', *Historia* 44 (1995), 120–1.

46. Livy may also discard suspense to warn us of impending disaster or pathos, or – as with the

cavalry skirmish discussed below – to reassure us, a technique also notable in Vergil: examples at Kraus (1994), 166 on 12.11.

47. In fact it occurs only three times in the decade, at beginning, middle (25.2.6), and end. (29.22.10 is an interpolation: S. P. Oakley, *CQ* 42 (1992), 547–51.)

48. Also called 'Einzelerzählungen' or 'individual narratives,' these are one of Livy's characteristic compositional units and the focus of much literary analysis since they were first identified (by K. Witte, 'Über die Form der Darstellung in Livius' Geschichtswerk', *RhM* 65 (1910), 270–305, 359–419); see further Oakley (1997), 125–8. For a sample analysis of an episode see above, pp. 62–70.

49. For the first two see below; for the annalistic material, see above, pp. 3–4, 7, Levene (1993) on prodigies, and Kraus (1994), 9–13. The standard model is that of Ginsburg (1981), whose view of Livy is, however, oversimplified; for a challenge to it see next n. but one.

50. 2.1.1 *Liberi iam hinc populi Romani res pace belloque gestas, annuos magistratus . . . peragam,* echoed at Tac. *A.* 1.1.1 *libertatem et consulatum L. Brutus instituit* (below, p. 94). See also T. P. Wiseman, *Remus* (Cambridge, 1995), 103.

51. 'Structuring Roman history: the consular year and the Roman historical tradition', *Histos* (23 October 1996).

52. For his play with traditional structures see e.g. Levene (1993), 38–42 (and often), Kraus (1994), 91 (on 6.1.8: reports of yearly elections).

53. The term is Oakley's (1997), 128. His discussion (111–51) of Livy's style, in which he treats nearly all of the elements discussed below, will become standard.

54. Livy's style was once thought to have become progressively more 'classical' after the highly poetic 'colouring' of the first books; this view has been modified, and most scholars now see him as adapting his language to the situation. On the variety and evolution of his style see Oakley (1997), 146–7.

55. 36. 10–11. Other close readings of Livy include Moles (1993); R. Jumeau, 'Remarques sur la structure de l'exposé livien', *RP* 65 (1939), 21–43; W. Jakel, 'Satzbau und Stilmittel bei Livius', *Gymnasium* 66 (1959), 302–17; T. J. Luce, 'Design and structure in Livy: 5.32–55', *TAPA* 102 (1971), 265–302; J. B. Solodow, 'Livy and the story of Horatius, 1.24–26', *TAPA* 109 (1979), 251–68.

56. Text and translation as in Walsh (1990), 26–9.

57. The next explicit narrative signpost, marking the start of the next season, comes at 12.1, 'at the beginning of spring' (*principio ueris*). On Livy's marking stages see Walsh (1961), 197–9; on chapter beginnings see Walsh (1990) on 12.1.

58. Examples at Kraus (1994), 101 on 6.2.14.

59. While the stratagem is conventional, Larisa's involvement suggests the Caesarian text. For Livy's use of and debt to Caesar see Oakley (1997), 129: 'it is a fact that the sentence-structure of no two other Latin historians is so alike.' For more complex examples of Livian intertextuality see above, n. 3 and Kraus (1994), 199–200 (on 6.18.5–15); for intertextuality in Tacitus see below, pp. 97–102.

60. Livy often moves the narrative 'lens' to follow a character; hence journeys, embassies, etc. become a means of making a transition from one part of the story to another. On the plot as a road see J. J. van Baak, *The Place of Space in Narration* (Amsterdam, 1983), 98, 118; on the transitional technique see Walsh (1961), 180–1.

61. For a general study of the word see J. Champeaux, '*Forte* chez Tite-Live', *REL* 45 (1967), 363–87.

62. For how to use campfires to mislead the enemy see Frontinus, *Strat.* 1.5.3, 22, 24, 2.5.17; for not being fooled see Kraus (1994), 183 on 6.15.7.

63. A further rounding off is obtained by the frame with another *praesidium*'s departure mentioned at 10.3: that was a Larisaean garrison that Antiochus released from Pherae (36.9.14–15).

64. The exception is the *ut*-clause at 10.4. On sieges in Livy see Walsh (1961), 191–7 and for an example just preceding our extract cf. 36.9.10–12. The capture of cities became the textbook example of a scene that cried out for the techniques of *euidentia* (above, n. 22; cf. Quint. 8.3.67–71): see Paul (1982) and N. Purcell, 'On the sacking of Carthage and Corinth', in Innes–Hine–Pelling (1995), 133–48.

65. For focalization (roughly equivalent to the concept of 'point of view'), a term coined by the French narratologist Gerard Genette, see D. Fowler, 'Deviant focalisation in Virgil's *Aeneid*', *PCPS* 36 (1990), 42–63 with references to earlier discussions.

66. Happy endings, such as we have here, produce a satisfying finale (as for instance in comedy); for emotions as a closural motif cf. also the last words of Sall. *BC* 61.9 *ita uarie per omnem exercitum laetitia maeror, luctus atque gaudia agitabantur* ('And so variously throughout the entire army happiness and sadness, grief and joy were stirred up') and see above, pp. 26–7.

67. This is an oft-told tale: references to its other occurrences are at Briscoe (1981), 235 on 11.1–4.

68. The idea that a king's subjects resemble him is conventional; here it explains the wholesale corruption and forgetfulness that overtake Antiochus' army (cf. also 5.28.4, 36.11.5 and the related motifs illustrated by Woodman (1977), 245 on Vell. 126.5).

69. For tense variation in historiography see Chausserie-Laprée (1969) especially 383–93 (on the combination perfect + imperfect, the reverse of the order we have here).

70. On the good general's eating habits cf. Vell. 41.2 *qui* [Julius Caesar] . . . *cibo in uitam non in uoluptatem uteretur* and Woodman (1983), 53–4 ad loc. Such a general also refrains from sleeping more than is necessary, so Antiochus' slumber doubly damns him. For Livy's interest in moral qualities see above, n. 44 and T. J. Moore, *Artistry and Ideology: Livy's Vocabulary of Virtue* (Frankfurt, 1989).

71. The computerized *Concordance to Livy* by D. W. Packard (Cambridge, Ma., 1968) revolutionized the study of Livian diction; searches for this chapter have been done using it, the Packard Humanities Institute CD-ROM of Latin literature, and the *TLL* (below, n. 83).

72. So for instance [Longinus], *On the Sublime* 8.1 (figures, diction, word arrangement): see D. Innes, 'Longinus, sublimity, and the low emotions', in Innes–Hine–Pelling (1995), 322 and n. 1.

73. For an introduction to the question of linguistic *decorum* (the kind of language that is 'fitting' in a given situation) see D. A. Russell, *Criticism in Antiquity* (Berkeley, 1981), 129–47, with 148–58 on 'Classification of Literature.' More on genre in F. Cairns, *Generic Composition in Greek and Latin Poetry* (Edinburgh, 1972) and G. B. Conte, *The Rhetoric of Imitation: Genre and Poetic Memory in Virgil and other Latin Poets* (Ithaca, 1986); for a recent theoretical discussion see T. O. Beebee, *The Ideology of Genre* (Pennsylvania, 1994).

74. There are some specialized studies of such language, in Livy and elsewhere: see H. Bruckmann, *Die römischen Niederlagen im Geschichtswerk des T. Livius* (Diss. Münster, 1938) on narratives of defeat; E. L. Wheeler, *Stratagem and the Vocabulary of Military Trickery* (Leiden, 1988); and more generally Walsh (1961), 191–204, Oakley (1997), 83–4.

75. The style, which uses short sentences, asyndeton (lack of connective particles), and passive verbs (often without the auxiliary *esse*) is not illustrated in our passage. It was identified by E. Fraenkel ('Eine Form römischer Kriegsbulletins', *Eranos* 54 (1956), 189–94); see Oakley (1997), 139 n. 146.

76. On the various formulae see Chausserie-Laprée (1969), 17–124 and above, n. 57 on the carefully marked stages.

77. E.g. at 37.17.7, 44.13.4; cf. also Cic. *Phil.* 13.11, Sil. 2.303 (both using the related verbs).

78. The expression has a metaphorical content, as both words can be used of water (the Larisaeans are tossing on waves); for the metaphor cf. Juv. 12.32, the Elder Sen. *C.* 1.1.10, Sen. *Medea* 939, Tac. *A.* 2.23.2, Apul. *Met.* 5.21. Before Livy, who uses it more than any other author, the combination is attested only at Lucr. 4.1077.

79. For Vergil's use see W. Clausen, ed., *Virgil Eclogues* (Oxford, 1994), 101 (on 3.38). The verb has isolated examples in Horace, Grattius, and Ovid, but is favoured by Livy (36x) and after him Curtius (27x), and by the technical writers Pliny the Elder (12x: natural science), Columella (10x: agriculture), Seneca the Younger (17x: philosophy and natural science), Celsus (11x: medicine), and Justinian (20x: law). This distribution (only in poetry before and contemporaneously with Livy; infrequently so afterward) suggests that his use of a choice term was then picked up and 'domesticated' by some imperial prose writers.

80. See Kraus (1994), 226 on 6.22.9.

81. Accius 435 Ribbeck; it does not appear to occur elsewhere outside Livy except at Frontinus *Strat.* 1.5.19, a story taken from Livy. It may be that the historian has borrowed the tragic expression on the model of a more usual phrase such as *fauces portus* ('the mouth of the harbour', *OLD fauces* 3a), again producing language that, while reminiscent of 'ordinary' military style, is in fact quite extraordinary.

82. See Briscoe (1981), 4.

83. Before this passage and 42.12.4 it is found at Cat. 64.302, Verg. *Aen.* 7.555; it then occurs

sporadically in imperial literature: see the citations at *Thesaurus Linguae Latinae* (Leipzig, 1900–) III.4.743.64–71.

84. This sentence is imitated by Tacitus at *H.* 4.36.2 *effusi in luxum et epulas et nocturnos coetus.*

85. See J. B. Hofmann and A. Szantyr, *Lateinische Grammatik.* Teil 2. *Lateinische Syntax und Stilistik* (Munich, 1965), 219; it is found with names of towns, islands, and regions (as here).

86. Scholars have always seen different levels in Livy's style, but his deliberate use of inconcinnity (lack of parallelism) in the Tacitean sense has been less commented on. See however J. L. Catterall, 'Variety and inconcinnity of language in the first decade of Livy', *TAPA* 49 (1938), 292–318 and Kraus (1994), 352 s.v. '*uariatio*' (Index).

87. That the two elements are parallel is guaranteed by the pair of comparative expressions (*latius quam pro ~ plures quam quot*); that pairing, in turn, further emphasizes the inconcinnity of the verb forms. For parallels to our sentence commentators cite 32.14.2 (*adortus . . . et . . . cum erexisset,* where editors often emend to *adortus est*); cf. the slightly different combinations at Tac. *H.* 2.34.2 (*simulantes . . . ac ne . . . . tereret*) and *A.* 3.3.1 (*rati . . . an ne . . . intellegerentur*), where see Woodman–Martin (1996), 90 ad loc. The combination of participle + *cum*-clause without the copulative particle is of course entirely regular.

88. One technical name for this device is *traductio* (also used for the repetition of a word in connecting sentences; see *OLD* 5 and von Albrecht (1989), 95, 97): for further examples see Kraus (1994), 353 s.v. 'word play' (Index).

89. The term comes from L. P. Wilkinson, *Golden Latin Artistry* (Cambridge, 1963), 167; his treatment of prose sentences (167–88) is perhaps the best and clearest available.

90. Had L. wanted to omit the first instance of the name, or combine the two clauses to remove the awkward use of the king in two different cases (*ad regem . . . consultanti*), he could easily have done so. This kind of parataxis is typical of early Latin prose; see von Albrecht (1989), 25 and 32.

91. The repetition of *uel* further elevates the tone; repetition of an initial word in sequential units either of verse or prose is called anaphora.

92. 'The anaphora of *nunc,* . . . originally poetical, was introduced into prose by Livy' (Martin–Woodman (1997), 213 on Tac. *A.* 4.51.1).

93. On this kind of arrangement, including discussion of shapes of *tricola,* see Kraus (1994), 21–4.

94. For 'iconic' language and Livy's use of postponement see Kraus (1994), 347 s.v. 'form ~ content' and 353 s.v. 'word order' (Index), and Oakley (1997), 141–2.

95. For technical studies of speech in Livy see R. Ullmann, *La Technique des discours dans Salluste, Tite Live, et Tacite* (Oslo, 1927) and *Étude sur le style des discours de Tite Live* (Oslo, 1929); A. Lambert, *Die indirekte Rede als Künstlerisches Stilmittel des Livius* (diss. Zürich, 1946); and J. Dangel, *La Phrase oratoire chez Tite-Live* (Paris, 1982); for more general discussions see Walsh (1961), 219–44 and Oakley (1997), 117–20, 139–41.

96. This sentence is singled out for criticism by Walsh (1990), 88 ('a much less elegant period-sentence than Livy's norm'); for other examples of 'strained' sentences in Livy see Oakley (1997), 132, quoting the lists made by the great nineteenth-century Livian scholars J. N. Madvig (*Kleine philologische Schriften* (Leipzig, 1875), 359–60) and O. Riemann (*Études sur la langue et la grammaire de Tite-Live* (Paris, [2]1885), 309–10).

97. The classic analysis of such periods is by M. Spilman, 'Cumulative sentence building in Latin historical narrative', *UCPCPh* 11 (1932), 153–247.

98. For the *phrase à relance* and other narrative sentence-types see Chausserie-Laprée (1969), 129–336.

99. Though this last *tricolon* consists only of nouns, they form an action-sequence within themselves: banquets with wine are followed by unspecified *uoluptates* (a polite periphrasis for sex) which are in turn followed by exhaustion and sleep. They can, therefore, be regarded as semi–continuative.

100. Galinsky (1996), 280–7; the quotations are from 283 and 286. Cf. also Ogilvie, *CHCL* 2.466: 'no other Roman historian was so inventive,' a remark which may not have been meant to be entirely complimentary.

101. Galinsky (1996), 284. The writer who in many ways is closest to Livy, both in time and in narrative technique (in the *Metamorphoses*), is Ovid, though Livy has none of the poet's pervasive iconoclastic cynicism; but the historian is nowhere near as humourless as he has been labelled (e.g. by P. G. Walsh, 'Livy's preface and the distortion of history', *AJP* 76 (1955), 371–4, Ogilvie ([2]1970), 4).

102. So for example Conte (1994), 370 (on the whole a surprisingly conservative and overstated treatment of Livy). The word frequently used to describe this overlap is 'anachronistic', but that misses the point.

103. Luce (1977), 230–97. He does not, however, seem to have thought that early Rome might have been radically different either in institutions or in ideals: see further the references at Kraus (1994), 28 n. 119.

104. On the levels of audience and spectacle in the *Ab urbe condita* see A. M. Feldherr, *Spectacle and Society in Livy's 'History'* (Diss. Berkeley, 1991); on internal deployment of *exempla* see Chaplin (1993).

105. He is also mentioned at 28.12.12, and may have been quoted in Book 59 (*perioch.* 59): Luce (1965), 209–10.

106. He probably inserted the digression in a second edition of the pentad: so Luce (1965), following a suggestion of Jean Bayet. For a recent discussion of 4.20, followed here, see Miles (1995), 40–7; for a new interpretation see J. W. Rich, *Chiron* 26 (1996), 85–127.

107. Miles (1995), 46.

108. Cf. the entertaining anecdote related by Suetonius about Pomponius Porcellus, the 'extraordinarily obnoxious overseer of the Latin language', who on one occasion objected to the emperor Tiberius' unusual diction on the grounds that while Tiberius could give citizenship to people he had not the power to do so to words (see Kaster (1995), 26–7, 226 on *Gramm.* 22.2).

109. There are very few cases of Augustus' censoring or punishing writers. One, Cassius Severus, was banished and his writings burned for 'unrestrained hostilities' (i.e. libel, apparently not directed against Augustus or his family but against leading senators); Ovid was exiled (presumably not primarily for his writing but for the mysterious *error*, possibly involvement with the *princeps'* adulterous granddaughter) but continued to publish; Timagenes, a Greek historian, was banished from Augustus' house but continued both to live in Rome and to attack the emperor. The older image of Augustus as repressive and tyrannous in his later years cannot be right: see K. A. Raaflaub and L. J. Samons III, 'Opposition to Augustus', in Raaflaub–Toher (1993), 417–54.

110. On his detachment see e.g. Conte (1994), 370, Galinsky (1996), 286 ('distance and independence of mind'), and see above, p. 10 on Sallust. Many of the ideas that Livy shared with Augustus had strong republican roots: see Kraus (1994), 8–9 and most recently Galinsky (1996), 284 ('the values that Augustus sought to restore were, after all, traditional ones. Livy, in his own way, was just as zealous in this regard as the *princeps'*) and 285 ('Like so many other Italians and Romans, Livy saw his own program take shape under Augustus . . . [who] actualized in the public aspirations that had been dormant'). For a judicious review of the problem of Livy and Augustus see E. Badin in *Livius: Aspekte seines Werkes*, ed. W. Schuller (Konstanz, 1993), 9–38.

111. He is interested above all in the exercise of power and to that end concentrates not only on the *res gestae* of the Roman military and political aristocracy but on the plebeian crowds as well; in this respect his history may have been quite radical; see R. T. Ridley, 'Patavinitas among the patricians? Livy and the conflict of the orders', in W. Eder, ed., *Staat und Staatlichkeit in der frühen römischen Republik* (Stuttgart, 1990), 132–3.

112. He 'remains the most nebulous figure of all the greater historians of the ancient world' (Walsh (1961), 1). He came from Padua in northern Italy, had at least one son, and worked in Rome, where he seems to have known Augustus and the future emperor Claudius (below, p. 99 n. 62); for what little more we know or can infer see further Kraus (1994), 1–4; for his dates see above, n. 2.

113. For the concept of the 'implied author' see Booth (²1983), 530 s.v. (Index).

114. The almost entirely unknown Gracchan historian Cn. Gellius may have written as much: Badian (1966), 11–12.

115. Kraus (1994), 1–2.

116. This is the historiographical topos *relata refero*, 'I tell the tale that I heard told' (see Kraus (1994), 206 on 6.18.16); Livy's frequent references to it are directly relevant to the notion that his history demands that we think not about what 'really' happened but about how and why the Roman traditions formed, and what they mean for the reader.

117. On these authorial interventions, with examples of many more, see R. B. Steele, 'The historical attitude of Livy', *AJP* 25 (1904), 15–44; on his mentions of contemporary Rome in the first decade see R. von Haehling, *Zeitbezüge des T. Livius in der ersten Dekade seines Geschichtswerkes* (1989).

118. Miles (1995), 47; on characters acting like historians see Kraus (1994), 149–51, 191, 213–14 (on Manlius Capitolinus) and Jaeger (1997), esp. on Septimus Marcius.

119. He was probably not the first such professional historian of Rome (see Wiseman (1987), 248–52 on Valerius Antias and others in the first century B.C.), but the Roman suspicion of intellectual activity for its own sake (above, p. 7) had not yet diminished, and the prejudice in favour of the 'senatorial historian' (i.e. the man who makes history and then retires to write it) was strong in the ancient world as in the modern; see further Earl (1965), 237–8, Kraus (1994), 5 n. 17.

120. Kraus (1994), 158 on 6.12.2–6; Miles (1995), 47–54.

121. 'The moralism of Plutarch's *Lives*', in Innes–Hine–Pelling (1995), 219–20.

122. A. Wallace-Hadrill, 'Time for Augustus', in M. Whitby, P. Hardie, and M. Whitby, edd., *Homo Viator* (Bristol, 1987), 221–30; see now also J. D. Evans, *The Art of Persuasion. Political Propaganda from Aeneas to Brutus* (Ann Arbor, 1992) and Galinsky (1996), 38–41.

123. Pelling (last n. but one, 207, 219) makes an analogy with the civic function of Greek tragedy, on which see the essays in J. J. Winkler and F. I. Zeitlin, edd., *Nothing to do with Dionysus? Athenian Drama in its Social Context* (Princeton, 1990).

124. E. T. Salmon, 'The evolution of Augustus' Principate', *Historia* 5 (1956), 456–78. For thoughtful discussions of the passage from republic to empire see W. Eder, 'Augustus and the power of tradition' in Raaflaub–Toher (1990), 71–122 and J. A. Crook, 'Augustus: power, authority, achievement' in A. K. Bowman, E. Champlin, and A. Lintott, edd., *The Cambridge Ancient History* Vol. X (^{2}1996), 113–46.

125. Miles (1995), 68.

IV. THE FIRST CENTURY A.D.

'The Roman historians subsequent to Livy', pronounced Sir Ronald Syme, 'have perished utterly.'[1] It is true that most of the historians who wrote in the century between Livy and Tacitus, whether well known (e.g. the elder Seneca and the elder Pliny) or less familiar (e.g. Servilius Nonianus and Fabius Rusticus), have survived only in fragments or not at all; but there are two exceptions, Velleius Paterculus and Curtius.

Velleius Paterculus

Velleius was born in (probably) 20 or 19 B.C. and began his career as military tribune around the turn of the millennium under the young Gaius Caesar in the east (101–102.1).[2] Perhaps in reaction to the trend of ever-larger works which culminated in Livy's 142 books, he wrote a summary history of Rome from its beginnings to A.D. 29 in two volumes.[3] Though we do not know exactly when he began to write, his dedication of the work to M. Vinicius, the consul of A.D. 30, indicates that publication was intended to be in the year of Vinicius' consulship.[4] Despite the slimness of his volumes (an impression exaggerated by the almost total loss of the first of them)[5] Velleius' work ranges extraordinarily widely. Though he becomes more expansive as he reaches his own times, and though in the later parts of his work he concentrates inevitably on the major protagonists (41–59.1 Caesar, 59.2–93 Augustus, 94–131 Tiberius),[6] in the earlier parts he treated Greek history as well as Roman and in digressions or excursuses he provides potted accounts of Roman colonization (1.14–15), Greek and/or Roman literature (1.16–18, 2.9, 36.2–3) and Roman provincialization (38–9). The juxtaposed digressions at the end of Book 1 (14–18) emphasize the break between his first and second volumes, the chronological moment for which is the fall of Carthage in 146 B.C. (1.12–13 ~ 2.1.1). In choosing this event as the decisive development in Rome's history Velleius follows Sallust (above, p. 21), by whose phraseology he was also greatly influenced;[7] but Velleius' general style has none of Sallust's famous jerkiness or abruptness (above, pp. 11–13), which he will have eschewed as being too subversive.[8]

Though Velleius' history of the republic is extremely useful and he often provides information found in no other source,[9] the defining experience of his life and career was his close association with the future emperor Tiberius on military campaign for nine continuous years between A.D. 4 and 12 (cf. 104.3). He served under Tiberius in Germany, Pannonia, and Dalmatia (104.3, 111.3, 114.2, 115.5) and as quaestor designate was in charge of a special mission for Tiberius in A.D. 6 (111.3). At one point he recalls the enthusiasm with which Tiberius was greeted by veterans in A.D. 4 after his return from Rhodes two years earlier (104.4): 'I was with you, general, in Armenia!'; 'I was in Raetia!'; 'I was decorated by you amongst the Vindelici!'; 'And I in Pannonia!'; 'And I in Germany!' It is difficult not to believe that these were also the feelings of Velleius himself, who at the time of Augustus' death in A.D. 14 had been designated praetor (along with his brother) for the following year (124.4). Certainly his enthusiasm for Tiberius shines out from the pages of his work and seems not to have been dimmed by his later experience in the senate, to whose ranks he will have been admitted by virtue of his quaestorship.

Velleius' career as soldier, senator, and magistrate qualifies him to be described as the kind of historian beloved by Syme: 'he had some of the advantages, we might say, of a Sallust or an Asinius Pollio over a Livy or a Fenestella'.[10] Yet Syme scorned Velleius' work and has been followed by the majority of modern historians, who, when dealing with Tiberius' principate, either dismiss Velleius with contempt or fail even to mention him at all.[11] Such practice almost defies belief. The years A.D. 14–29 are one of the relatively few periods of ancient history for which we have the eye-witness report of a contemporary participant in events. Velleius' work, though naturally no less rhetorical or partial than that of any other ancient historiographer, should be prized rather than proscribed by modern historians; but his fault is that he puts forward a different view from that of the cynical Tacitus (below, pp. 103–9). Tacitus himself acknowledged that malice masquerades as free speech (H. 1.1.2), and, since we are all in favour of free speech, any contrary view to Tacitus' must be damned as servile panegyric.[12]

Velleius' account of Tiberius provides vital evidence for the establishment view of events, while his attitude to the *princeps* helps to explain the long survival of the imperial system of government. It would nevertheless be mistaken to suppose that the darker developments of Tiberius' principate left no mark on Velleius' text. His treatment of Sejanus (127–8), so far from being a facile eulogy of the man, is an uneasy defence of the emperor's promotion of an unpopular helper;[13] and the narrative ends, not (as might have been expected) on a climactic note, but with an anguished summary of treason and death (130.3–5) and an anxious prayer for the preservation of things (131).[14] As with Tacitus, we have to read between the lines, a procedure for which, in the case of Velleius, most modern historians have shown a conspicuous reluctance.[15]

Curtius

There is dispute over Curtius' identity, and hence over his dates, but many scholars assume that he is the Curtius Rufus whose vision of a ghost is reported by the younger Pliny in a famous letter (7.27.2–3) and by Tacitus in the *Annals* under A.D. 47 (11.20.3–21.3). This man was suffect consul in A.D. 43,[16] and later, as the ghost had allegedly predicted, proconsul of Africa, where he died. A man of the same name, who is mentioned as a rhetorician by Suetonius, is likely to be identical with the visionary and hence also with the historian.[17]

Curtius' claim to literary fame rests upon his history of Alexander the Great, written originally in ten books but now lacking Books 1–2 and parts of Books 5, 6 and 10. That the young Macedonian conqueror exercised a fascination upon the Romans is clear from Livy's famous 'Alexander digression' (9.17–19),[18] from the *suasoriae* of the elder Seneca in which Alexander features (1 and 4), and from Alexander's imitation by numerous politicians and emperors.[19] When Catullus in Poem 11 begins his 'travelogue' with India (lines 2–4) and ends it with 'great Caesar' (10 *Caesaris . . . magni*), his contemporary readers will have appreciated instantly that allusion was being made to Alexander, who was famous for having reached India and for being called 'the Great'. Curtius' narrative was likewise designed to appeal to an established tradition.

Curtius' work is invariably described as 'Livian' and 'rhetorical', the latter a prelude to its summary dismissal. What these terms mean, and whether they are justified, may be seen from a representative passage (4.4.19–21):

Tyros septimo mense quam oppugnari coepta erat capta est, urbs et uetustate originis et crebra fortunae uarietate ad memoriam posteritatis insignis. condita ab Agenore, diu mare non uicinum modo sed quodcumque classes eius adierunt dicionis suae fecit. et, si famae libet credere, haec gens litteras prima aut docuit aut didicit; coloniae certe eius paene orbe toto diffusae sunt: Carthago in Africa, in Boeotia Thebae, Gades ad Oceanum. credo libero commeantes mari saepiusque adeundo ceteris incognitas terras elegisse sedes iuuentuti, quae tunc abundabat,[20] siue quia crebris motibus terrae (nam hoc quoque traditur) cultores eius fatigati, noua et externa domicilia armis sibimet quaerere cogebantur. multis ergo casibus defuncta et post excidium renata nunc tandem longa pace cuncta refouente sub tutela Romanae mansuetudinis acquiescit.

Tyre was taken in the seventh month after it had started to be attacked, a city outstanding in the memory of posterity both for its origin's antiquity and for the frequent variety of its fortune. Founded by Agenor, for a long time it imposed its jurisdiction not only on the neighbouring sea but on whichever one its fleets reached. And, if there is attraction in believing the legend, this people was the first either to teach or to learn writing; its colonies at least were spread over almost all the world: Carthage in Africa, in Boeotia Thebes, Cadiz by the Ocean. I believe that, as they criss-crossed the open sea, and quite often reaching lands unknown to everyone else, they chose settlements for their young men, who abounded at the time; or else its inhabitants, because they were worn out with the frequent earthquakes (for this too is reported), were compelled to seek by arms new and foreign homes for themselves. Having experienced, then, many circumstances and being reborn after its destruction, now at last the city – given the general revival of the Long Peace – rests under the protection of Roman humaneness.

This is the conclusion of Curtius' well-known description of the siege of Tyre, which took place in 332 B.C.[21] After an opening sentence (derived from Livy 21.15.3 'in the eighth month after it had started to be attacked, Saguntum was taken') on the duration of the siege, Curtius appends an appositional phrase in the manner of Livy (cf. 5.22.8, 24.41.7, 31.29.11) to describe the city's outstanding reputation (*ad memoriam insignis* is twice used by Livy, at 7.28.9 and 24.49.8).[22] Two reasons are given, of which the second (the frequent variety of its fortune) is surely intended to remind the reader that fluctuating fortunes are the essence of historiographical narrative (the classic example is Cic. *Fam.* 5.12.4–5).

Thus Curtius begins the passage by making it clear that he is about to praise the city of Tyre. Now Quintilian, the professor of rhetoric who was a much younger contemporary of Curtius, observes in his discussions of 'how to praise' that 'cities are praised in the same way as men: the founder takes the place of the parent, and antiquity [*uetustas*] carries great authority' (3.7.26). The reference to antiquity at once explains the eulogistic nature of *uetustate originis* ('its origin's antiquity') in Curtius' opening sentence, which in turn is explained by Tyre's foundation by Agenor at the start of the next sentence (Agenor taking 'the place of the parent'). Curtius then reports the story of Tyre's pioneering role (*prima*, 'first') in the development of writing: this conforms exactly to the notion that 'what most pleases an audience is the celebration of deeds which our hero was the first [*primus*] . . . to perform' (Quint. 3.7.16). The story of priority is enhanced by the qualification suggested in *si famae libet credere* ('if there is attraction in believing the legend'), which itself is expressed in Livian language (*libet credere* occurs five times in Livy).[23]

The widespread diffusion of Tyrian colonies from Boeotia to Cadiz perhaps alludes to the panegyrical commonplace that the hero 'rules from east to west'; likewise the opening-up of previously unknown territory is a well-worn motif of panegyric.[24] Curtius offers two suggested reasons for Tyrian colonization: the first is expressed in Livian language (cf. Liv. 23.49.12 *iuuentute abundante*, 'young men abounding'), while the parenthesis in the second is also Livian (especially 1.31.4 *nam id quoque traditur*, 'for that too is reported'; also 2.18.4 *id quoque enim traditur*). The passage as a whole is then concluded by a sentence which looks back to the first: the metaphor of rebirth (*renata*) recalls Liv. 6.1.3 *renatae urbis* ('the reborn city'),[25] while that of resting (*acquiescit*) recalls Liv. 5.23.12 *acquiesceret ciuitas* ('the state might rest').

Thus the evidence of this passage fully supports the standard view of Curtius: he exhibits even more indebtedness to Livy than scholars have recognized, and not only is he 'rhetorical' but he actually follows the rules of rhetoric as set down by a professor of the subject. Neither feature is a ground for blame. In the ancient world the writing of history was a literary pursuit, so it is as normal for Curtius to imitate Livy as it is for Vergil to imitate Homer. Livy's 142 volumes were the preeminent product of earlier historiography, and it would be strange indeed if a first-century historian were not thoroughly acquainted with, and anxious to display his admiration for, Livy's masterpiece.

As for 'rhetorical', this is a much abused term in modern discussions of ancient historians and it acquires added piquancy in Curtius' case if he was indeed a professional rhetorician (above, p. 84). Yet Curtius is of course no different from other ancient historians, all of whom were rhetorical (above, pp. 5–6). His final words on Tyre amount to an obituary notice for the city,[26] and he should no more be condemned for this and similar flourishes than Tacitus, who in his *Histories* writes an obituary for the Capitol at Rome (below, p. 96).

NOTES

1. Syme (1958), 358.
2. References to chapters 19–131 of Book 2 usually dispense with the book number. For a detailed study of Velleius' career see Sumner (1970).

3. For the summary nature of Velleius' work and its relative novelty see Woodman (1975), esp. 275–87. Note also R. J. Starr, 'The scope and genre of Velleius' history', *CQ* 31 (1981), 162–74.

4. Woodman (1975), 273–5.

5. We lack the preface and his account of everything between the time of Romulus (1.8.4–6) and the battle of Pydna in 168 B.C. (1.9).

6. For this trend see Woodman (1977), 30–50; also above, pp. 32–3.

7. See A. J. Woodman, *Hommages à M. Renard* (Brussels, 1968), 1.785–99.

8. For this theme see *RICH*, 140–6.

9. See Woodman (1983), 287 s.v. Velleius Paterculus (c).

10. Sumner (1970), 279. (Fenestella was an antiquarian writer contemporary with Livy; his work survives only in fragments.) Syme, who took Pollio as his model and inspiration for *The Roman Revolution* (see pp. vii–viii, 6–7), valued Sallust, Pollio and especially Tacitus for their experience of political affairs: see e.g. Syme (1939), 5 and 420, and esp. 'The senator as historian' in *Ten Studies in Tacitus* (Oxford, 1970), 1–10. Syme's view thus has something in common with that of Polybius, for whom practical experience was an important element in what he called 'pragmatic history': see Walbank (1972), 56 and 66–96.

11. For Syme see e.g. *RP*, 3.1090–1104; other exx. in Woodman (1975), 289 and *RICH*, 213 n. 34. An honourable exception is Sumner (1970).

12. See further *RICH*, 203–6. Tacitus' point remains current today: 'the selection of "good" news [is] propaganda . . . only "bad" news is objective' (ironical letter in *The Times*, 30 April 1993).

13. See Woodman (1977), 245–8. On Sejanus see also below, pp. 103–8.

14. See Woodman (1977), 272–6.

15. Yet Syme himself had warned that 'It is the mark of political literature under the Empire . . . that it should not carry its meaning on its face' (1958, 29).

16. See *RP*, 3.1434 n. 90.

17. See Kaster (1995), 336–7.

18. This digression is drawn upon by Curtius: see the evidence reported by P. Moore, *Q. Curtius Rufus' Historiae Alexandri Magni: a Study in Rhetorical Historiography* (Diss. Oxford, 1994), 198–206.

19. See e.g. Woodman (1983), 214–15 with further references.

20. The transmitted text reads *qua tunc abundabat*, which Zarotus corrected to *abundabant*; but *quae* is perhaps supported by Liv. 23.49.12 (see p. 86).

21. The description begins at 4.2.1 and has been analysed by W. Rutz, 'Zur Erzählungskunst des Q. Curtius Rufus: Die Belagerung von Tyrus', *Hermes* 95 (1965), 570–82.

22. Note, however, that the phrase was used earlier (though differently) by Cicero (*Dom.* 43), who also has *memoria posteritatis* thrice (*Rab. Post.* 16, *Mil.* 97, *Phil.* 9.7).

23. *si famae credimus* is at Liv. 1.49.9, but similar phraseology also appears elsewhere (e.g. Luc. 3.220 *famae si creditur*, again of the Phoenicians and writing).

24. See Woodman (1977), 241 and 142–3 respectively.

25. It is, however, worth noting that *Roma Renata Renascens* appears on the coinage of (among others) Galba: see *OLD renascor* 1a.

26. There is also an obituary notice for Persepolis at 5.7.8–9.

V. TACITUS

Beginnings and endings

The younger Pliny in one of his letters repeats a story which had been told to him by Tacitus (*Ep.* 9.23.2–3):

I have never derived more pleasure than from a recent exchange with Cornelius Tacitus. He was saying that a Roman knight had sat next to him at the last races: after various learned exchanges he had asked 'Are you Italian or provincial?', and Tacitus had replied 'You know me – from your reading'. To this he had said 'Are you Tacitus or Pliny?'

Engaging though it is to visualize the seemingly austere historian as a racing devotee, Pliny's delight at the knight's uncertainty was perhaps not reciprocated by Tacitus. Nevertheless Pliny elsewhere makes out that the two authors were fellow spirits and the best of friends (*Ep.* 7.20.4), and it is from references in Pliny's correspondence that we know the period during which Tacitus was writing his *Histories*.

In two of his most famous letters Pliny responds to a request from Tacitus for information concerning the eruption of Vesuvius in A.D. 79, which had killed Pliny's uncle (*Ep.* 6.16 and 20); conversely, convinced that Tacitus' *Histories* will be immortal and thus anxious to feature in them himself (*Ep.* 7.33.1), Pliny volunteers to Tacitus inside information about an episode in A.D. 93, of which Tacitus will be aware already in general terms (*Ep.* 7.33.3). From such references it may be inferred that Tacitus was at work on the *Histories* in the years A.D. 106–8.[1]

The *Histories* shares with the Old Testament and St John's Gospel the fact that it begins with the word 'Beginning':

Initium mihi operis Seruius Galba iterum Titus Vinius consules erunt.

The beginning of my work will be the consulships of Servius Galba (for the second time) and Titus Vinius.

But, whereas the evangelist and the author of Genesis refer to the beginning of their respective stories, Tacitus refers only to the beginning of his work, as we learn two words later (*operis*). The beginning of his work is not necessarily the beginning of his story. Tacitus' next six words tell us what the beginning of his work consists of: the year when Servius Galba and Titus Vinius were consuls (i.e. A.D. 69). But, when we reach the very last word of the sentence, we see that the verb is future (*erunt*): the beginning, which we seemed promised at the beginning of the sentence (and of the book), is not after all the beginning of the work itself, which evidently lies ahead in the text. The beginning which we have been given, and which begins with the word 'Beginning', is in fact the beginning of something else: Tacitus' preface.[2]

The preface to the *Histories* is an elaborate affair. The next paragraph (1.1.3–4) begins with the statement that Tacitus had no personal connection with the man whose second consulship will open his work (*Mihi Galba . . .*, 'To me Galba . . .', picking up the first sentence of the preface); he then extends this statement to cover Otho and Vitellius, before acknowledging that his political career had been helped along by Vespasian, Titus, and Domitian, all of whom he nevertheless intends to treat impartially.[3] The paragraph ends as follows:

If my life lasts, I have reserved the principate of Divine Nerva and the command of Trajan, more productive and safer material, for my old age, given the rare fertility of a climate in which it is allowed to think what you want and to say what you think.

Two points are to be noted. First, readers now know that the narrative of the *Histories* will end with Domitian (and presumably with his death in A.D. 96). Second, Tacitus' promise to write a future work on the reigns of Nerva and Trajan qualifies what he had said in the preface to an earlier work, his biography of his father-in-law Julius Agricola. There Tacitus had contrasted the reign of Domitian with those of Nerva and Trajan (*Agr.* 2–3) and had promised to write a future work on both periods, present and past (*Agr.* 3.3):

It will nevertheless be no displeasure . . . to compose a memorial of previous slavery and a testimony of present advantages.

The *Agricola* appeared around A.D. 98; a decade later the narrative of Nerva and Trajan is still in the future, while his account of Domitian forms the finale of a work which has extended further back into the past.

The third paragraph of the *Histories'* preface (1.2–3) begins with the sentence 'The work [*Opus*] I am approaching is rich [*opimum*] in disasters, grim with battles, riven with rebellion and savage even during peace itself'. Here *Opus* looks back to *operis* at the very start of the preface, while *opimum* sustains the agricultural metaphor which Tacitus introduced with *uberiorem* ('more productive') in the previous sentence.[4] The paragraph as a whole constitutes a foretaste of, or 'blurb' for, all the gripping events which Tacitus will describe in his work:[5] for the verb 'I am approaching' (*adgredior*) warns us at the start that the preface is still in progress and that Tacitus has not yet reached the work proper (*opus*).

Further delay in starting his work is announced by Tacitus at the start of the next section of the preface (1.4.1):

Yet, before I compose my intended subject, it seems necessary to retrace the state of the City, the intention of the armies, the attitude of the provinces, the elements of strength and weakness across the world as a whole . . .

Before he starts, Tacitus is obliged to go back; and, just as his retrospective survey begins at 1.4.2 with an 'end' (namely Nero's death: '*Finis* Neronis . . .'), so it ends at 1.11.3 with a reference back to the beginning (of the book):

This was the state of Roman affairs when Servius Galba (for the second time) and Titus Vinius were consuls and initiated [*inchoauere*] a year which was the last [*ultimum*] for them and almost terminal [*supremum*] for the commonwealth.

The word-for-word repetition of the consuls' names indicates that we have at last reached the beginning which we were promised at the start of the book; but this beginning not only is not the beginning of the story, which the retrospective survey has already provided, but it also initiates (*inchoauere*) an ending: it is an ending for the two consuls themselves (*ultimum*), because they would both be killed before a month of A.D. 69 was completed, and almost for the state too (*supremum*), because the war with which Tacitus is about to begin his work was a civil war.[6]

In this preface Tacitus' manipulation of beginnings and endings is not simply verbal wit[7] but reflects or underlines the fact (of which the *Histories* is itself a very good example) that it is difficult to begin a story. Modern readers have often wondered why Tacitus did not begin either with Nero's death in June A.D. 68 or with Vespasian's accession in July A.D. 69, both of which have seemed to some to be more natural beginnings.[8] Syme, on the other hand, believed that, given the complications of the period, Tacitus' starting-point was 'vital and inevitable';[9] others have believed that Tacitus wished to impose a strictly annalistic format, replete with the republican resonances associated with consular years (above, p. 62), on subject matter which is quintessentially imperial. Whatever the truth,[10] Tacitus' manipulations draw attention to the issue, while his retrospective survey means that he characteristically enjoys the best of both worlds (see also above, p. 16).

'In his old age Tacitus turned again to history';[11] but despite the promises issued in the prefaces of the *Agricola* and *Histories*, Tacitus' next work was an account, not of Nerva and Trajan, but of the emperors from Tiberius to Nero. Instead of moving forwards, the historian has again moved further back in time. No explanation for this is offered in the preface to the *Annals*, which in brevity and directness contrasts starkly with the preface to the *Histories*. The last sentence of the *Annals'* preface sets out Tacitus' programme for the rest of his work (1.1.3):[12]

inde consilium mihi pauca de Augusto et extrema tradere, mox Tiberii principatum et cetera, sine ira et studio, quorum causas procul habeo.

Therefore my intention is to relate a few things about Augustus, and his final period, then Tiberius' principate and the rest, without anger and enthusiasm, the reasons for which I hold at a distance.

The phrase *pauca de Augusto* corresponds to the first brief section of narrative from 1.2.1 (*Postquam Bruto . . .*) to 1.4.1 (where there is a reference to Augustus' continuing good health); *extrema* corresponds to the second brief section from 1.4.2 (where there are references to Augustus' old age, physical decline, and approaching death) to 1.5.4 (where the news of his death is released); *Tiberii principatum* refers to the Tiberian narrative as a whole, from 1.6.1 ('The first act of the *new principate* was . . .') to the emperor's obituary notice at the end of Book 6 (51); *cetera* refers to the remainder of the work.

Most readers have acclaimed Tacitus' decision to begin his main narrative in mid-A.D. 14 with the accession of Tiberius, since the accession established the dynastic principle on which the empire was based; but Sir Ronald Syme, who defended the start of the *Histories*, consistently maintained that Tacitus himself came to regret his starting-point in the *Annals* and to believe that he should have started a decade earlier in A.D. 4.[13] Though Syme's point has not met with general agreement, Tacitus in *Annals* 3 does indicate that the emperor Augustus will feature in a future work (24.3):

I shall recall the rest of that period if, after completing what I have intended, I extend my life to further concerns.

But Tacitus never turned to those future concerns: on his death (at an unknown date) his major contribution to historiography consisted of the *Histories* and *Annals*, which, in reverse order, together covered the years A.D. 14–96.

Neither of these works has survived complete to this day. Each breaks off in mid-sentence, the *Annals* in Book 16 (35.2) in A.D. 66,[14] the *Histories* in Book 5 (26.3) in A.D. 70. Though we are told by St Jerome that both works together amounted to thirty books,[15] we know neither how many books each work contained or even what the original title of each work was: Vertranius in his edition of 1569 was the first modern scholar to divide and title the works as we now have them.[16] *Annals* 11–16 and *Histories* 1–5 are numbered consecutively from *XI* to *XXI* by the single manuscript on which their survival depends,[17] and some scholars have indeed believed that the *Annals* originally comprised no more than sixteen books;[18] yet the six-book (or hexadic) structure, so clear in Tacitus' narratives of Tiberius (*A.* 1–6) and of Gaius and Claudius (*A.* 7–12), was almost certainly maintained for Nero,[19] the beginning of whose narrative (13.1.1) is an 'action replay' of that of Tiberius.[20] And, if the *Annals* originally comprised eighteen books, it follows from St Jerome's statement that the *Histories* will have comprised twelve.[21]

Whatever the case, it is striking that Tacitus' initial promise in the *Agricola* that he would write an account of Nerva and Trajan was not fulfilled by the *Histories*, which exhibits a modified version of that promise, and that this modified version in turn was not fulfilled by the *Annals*, which contains an entirely new promise and is deafeningly silent about Trajan in the surviving books.[22] Tacitus' repeated retreat from his own age in favour of ever more distant material carries the suggestion (which may of course be as false as it is intentional) that the reigns of Nerva and Trajan did not justify in practice one of the very grounds on which the historian had commended them in theory: namely that the reigns contrasted with that of Domitian and offered the opportunity for free speech and thought.

Tacitus' promise in the *Agricola* suggests, and the *Panegyric* of his friend Pliny confirms, that Trajan's reign (even if not the brief interlude of Nerva) demanded comparison with Domitian;[23] but Tacitus' decision to close the *Histories* with Domitian's death precludes any such contrast. It might be argued that, since the tone of Tacitean historiography is largely critical, his account of the years A.D. 14–96 is intended as implicit praise of Trajan. As Pliny said, 'a living emperor is best praised if his predecessors are criticized according to their deserts' (*Pan.* 53.6). Yet this implication seems excluded by the author himself, since Tacitus prefaces each work by testifying to the impartiality of his treatment (*H.* 1.1.3, *A.* 1.1.3): there is thus no professedly critical stance from which approval of the present may be inferred.

Is it, then, the case that Tacitus' account of A.D. 14–96 serves as disguised criticism of the present?[24] Syme held the interdependent beliefs that Tacitus' writing career extended into the reign of Hadrian and that the *Annals* exhibits allusions to that ruler:[25] not many scholars have been convinced, but that is not to say that he does not allude to

Trajan and other contemporaries ('all history is contemporary history').[26] A coeval of both Tacitus and Pliny was the satirist Juvenal, whose first book (*Satires* 1–5) also belongs to Trajan's reign. Juvenal's indignation at contemporary society, expressed forcefully at the opening of the first satire, seems to fizzle out lamely at the end, where for diplomatic reasons he promises that he will attack only the dead (1.170–1).[27] Yet it is not to be doubted that behind Juvenal's victims lurk contemporary personalities,[28] and Tacitus himself, in the remarkable digression with which he concludes the year A.D. 24, says that readers for their part often suspect double meanings even when they are not intended (*A.* 4.33.4):

> You will find those who, on account of a similarity of behaviour, think that others' misdeeds are being imputed to themselves; even glory and virtue [*gloria ac uirtus*] have enemies, as being too close an indictment of their opposites.

Here Tacitus, echoing the language used by Sallust when he too discussed the problems of the reader's responses (above, p. 14), implicitly claims a lack of intent on his own part;[29] but many readers may feel that the claim is disingenuous.

This digression is used by Tacitus to emphasize the separation of one year's narrative from the next,[30] yet the new year begins with an episode which sustains the theme of double readings: the historian Cremutius Cordus was charged in A.D. 25 with having praised Brutus and Cassius in his history, praise which was alleged by vindictive contemporaries to denote criticism of the imperial régime (4.34–5).[31] Such interplay between closure and continuity is typical of much ancient writing[32] but especially of annalistic historiography, which generally consists of a series of self-contained narrative units, each of them based on the events of a single year.[33] Annalistic units may vary greatly in length: six years (A.D. 23–8) are compressed into *Annals* 4, for example, whereas a single year (A.D. 69) extends over almost three and a half books of the *Histories* (1.11.3–4.37.3). Likewise Tacitus varies the arrangement of events within each individual year:[34] though the 'Livian' pattern of events (domestic–foreign–domestic) predominates in the Tiberian hexad of the *Annals*, years consisting exclusively of domestic events are found as well and come to predominate in the Neronian books, which, in the case of A.D. 58, also exhibit a year of unique complexity (*A.* 13.34–58: domestic–foreign–domestic–foreign–domestic). Similar differences are evident in the counterpoint of book and narrative year. Three of the extant Tiberian books (*A.* 2, 4 and 5) begin with the start of a new year, the one genuine exception (*A.* 3) clearly intended to emphasize the continuing significance of the Germanicus story;[35] but four of the extant later books (*A.* 12, 13, 15 and 16) begin with a year already in progress, although the one exception (*A.* 14) opens as arrestingly as all but one of the others.[36] In addition, Book 12 shares with Book 6 the phenomenon of an annalistic unit which, as Tacitus explicitly says, incorporates the events of more than a single year (cf. 6.38.1, 12.40.5).

The competing claims of closure and continuity are well illustrated by the first three books of the Tiberian hexad. Book 1 of the *Annals* begins famously as follows: *Vrbem Romam a principio reges habuere. libertatem et consulatum L. Brutus instituit* ('The City of Rome from its beginning was held by kings. Freedom and the consulship were established by L. Brutus'). In the space of a dozen words Tacitus has summarized two and a half centuries of Roman history, a period which it took Livy the whole of his first book to describe. Yet, despite such compression, Tacitus' words could have been fewer: since the consulship embodied freedom by definition, as Livy himself said (2.1.1, 7–8), there seems no need for the doublet 'freedom and the consulship'. The reason, however, become clear at the end of Book 1 (81.1–2):

About the consular elections which occurred then, for the first time in his principate, and thereafter, I would dare to vouch for scarcely anything: . . . such things were mere verbal display, empty of substance – or deceptive – and, the more impressive their covering in the guise of freedom, poised to erupt in an all the more dangerous servitude.

Here we have the counterpart to the beginning of the book. *Annals* 1 begins with the transition from monarchy (*reges*) to freedom and the consulship (*libertatem et consulatum*); it ends with Tacitus' casting doubt on Tiberius' good faith over the consular elections and maintaining that his specious words of freedom would lead to a worse servitude (*seruitium*). The grim framework of Book 1 marks the route from freedom and the republican consulship at the beginning to the imperial consular elections and slavery at the end. This is the opposite route to that travelled by the reader of Livy's first book, which begins with Rome's first king and ends with the establishment of freedom and the consulship (1.60.3 *liberatam . . . duo consules*).[37]

Annals 2 ends with a pair of paragraphs, in the first of which Tiberius intervenes helpfully in a grain crisis (87):

Yet he did not on that account adopt the designation of 'Parent of his Country' which was proffered (as before), and he bitterly rebuked those who had called his occupations 'divine' and himself 'master'. Hence speech was confined and slippery [*lubrica*] under a princeps who dreaded freedom but hated sycophancy.

The cross-reference 'as before' relates to an episode four years earlier near the end of Book 1 (72.1):

Tiberius rejected the name of 'Father of his Country' which had been thrust upon him quite often by the people; . . . insisting that all humanity's affairs were uncertain and that, the more he acquired, the more slippery his ground [*in lubrico*].

On this earlier occasion Tiberius had defended his rejection of the title with a moderate statement in which he applied to himself the metaphor *lubricus*. On the later occasion at the end of Book 2 Tacitus throws the metaphor back at him, using *lubricus* to describe the emperor's inhibiting effect on people's capacity to speak and adding a sardonic comment about freedom.[38]

It is freedom which links the penultimate with the final paragraph of Book 2, an obituary notice of the German chief Arminius (88). A rival chief had promised to kill Arminius, if the Romans provided a suitable poison; but Tiberius demurred, saying that 'the Roman people avenged their enemies not by treachery or concealment but openly and armed', a statement which Arminius, who had served in the Roman army, had earlier applied to himself (1.59.3 'he conducted war not by betrayal . . . but openly against armed men'). Tacitus continues the obituary by saying that Arminius aimed at kingship amongst the Germans but found his compatriots desiring freedom, and he was eventually killed by relatives who used deceitful methods, the like of which the Romans had earlier declined. Whereupon Tacitus concludes with this impressive tribute (88.2): 'the liberator of Germany without doubt . . . ambivalent in battles but not defeated in war'. Yet, while the latter part of this tribute, by echoing a long-standing boast of the Romans themselves,[39] seems to endorse Arminius' own earlier claim to Roman standards of conduct, the former part, by its proximity to the statement of the man's kingly ambitions, seems to question the nature of his commitment to freedom.

Book 3 of the *Annals* opens with Agrippina on the high seas, returning to Rome with the ashes of her dead husband, Germanicus; at his subsequent burial, which is vividly described, the people allude to his republicanism (3.4.1) and call Agrippina the one remaining token of the past (3.4.2). The book ends with the funeral of the aged Junia, who, as wife of Cassius and sister of Brutus, personified the long-lost days of the republic (3.76).[40] Thus the end of Book 3 not only mirrors the beginning but is linked to the ends of the two previous books by describing the loss of a symbol of freedom.[41]

The deaths which close *Annals* 2 and 3 illustrate the obvious point that death is a natural termination for a book, an impressive example of which is the sequence which ends *Histories* 3. The first death is that of Fabius Valens (62.1), whose head is severed and who receives an obituary notice (62.2). The next man to die is Flavius Sabinus (74.2), whose head is also severed and who also receives an obituary notice (75.1–2). Between these two Tacitus describes the burning of the temple of Jupiter on the Capitol (71), and the temple too receives an obituary notice (71.4–72.3).[42] The destruction of the Capitol was itself a form of decapitation, as both its name and the circumstances of its foundation suggest. Livy, who tells the story first at 1.55.5–6, makes Camillus repeat it in the speech with which Book 5 closes (54.7): 'Here is the Capitol, where once upon a time, on the discovery of a human head [*capite*], the prophetic reply was given that in that place would be the head [*caput*] of government'. Thus the destruction of the Capitol denoted the destruction of the metaphorical head of the body politic, a metaphor activated by the adjacent contexts: 'buried metaphors provide the conceptual logic underlying historical narrative'.[43] It is a graphic symbol of the suicide which is civil war, and one which Tacitus had already singled out in his 'blurb' for the work (*H.* 1.2.1 'the Capitol itself burned at the citizens' hands': see above, p. 89).

After Camillus' speech Livy ends his first pentad on the optimistic note of rebuilding which will be resumed at the start of the next (5.55.1–5 and 6.1.1–3);[44] but Tacitus has still another death to record, that of Vitellius (85), the last of the Four Emperors to die in the civil wars, who also will receive an obituary notice (86.1–2). The climactic nature of his death is marked by references back to the deaths of Flavius Sabinus and, earlier, of Galba (1.41.2–3, 49.1),[45] another decapitated figure, whose killing Tacitus had associated with the near-termination of the commonwealth itself at the start of the work (1.11.3: above, p. 90). Yet, despite this climax, Tacitus' next book begins characteristically with an end rather than a beginning (*H.* 4.1.1): 'With Vitellius killed, it was rather that war had ceased than peace begun'.

When Cicero was urging Lucceius to write a monograph on the Catilinarian conspiracy (above, p. 18), he assumed that his friend would have no problem in excerpting the subject 'from your continuous writings, in which you cover the unbroken history [*perpetuam . . . historiam*] of events' (*Fam.* 5.12.6). On the other hand, the Cambridge medievalist F. W. Maitland wrote that 'Such is the unity of all history that any one who endeavours to tell a piece of it must feel that his first sentence tears a seamless web'.[46] Tacitus in his *Histories* and *Annals* was obliged to make such tears, but his repeated manipulation of beginnings and endings suggests that he was scarcely insensitive to the seamlessness of history's web.

Intertextuality[47]

Augustus' death at the start of the *Annals* is shortly followed by a double mutiny (1.16–52), which is likened to civil war (1.16.1, 19.3, 49.1)[48] and thus foreshadows the civil war that will erupt on Nero's death at the end of the *Annals* and had been described by Tacitus himself already in the *Histories*.[49] Indeed the notion of civil war is recalled by metaphor and motif throughout the work, as if to suggest that the principate established by Augustus 'is constantly in danger of perishing by the same violent means through which it came to power'.[50] Moreover, the mutiny in *Annals* 1 is followed by events in Germany (1.61–5) which are modelled by Tacitus on episodes in his own earlier *Histories* (2.70, 5.14–15).[51] Thus the *Annals*, besides constituting an oblique commentary on Tacitus' time of writing (above, pp. 92–3), looks to its own more immediate future as well as to the more recent past from which the principate had sprung.[52]

Yet within the pages of the *Annals* there live figures from a more distant era too. Sejanus, possessing a daring spirit (4.1.3 *animus audax*) and aiming at monarchy (*parando regno*), is famously the reincarnation of Sallust's Catiline (*BC* 5.4 *animus audax*, 6 *dum sibi regnum pararet*); Poppaea Sabina (13.45.3) recalls Sallust's Sempronia (*BC* 25.3–5); Vatinius, a prodigy (*ostentum*) with a wretched background and physical deformity who puts on a gladiatorial display for Nero (15.34.2), resembles the homonym attacked by Cicero as an evil omen (*auspicium malum*) with a wretched background and facial swelling, who puts on an illegal gladiatorial display (*Vat.* 17, 37, 39).[53] When Tacitus begins the story of the accused historian Cremutius Cordus (4.34.1 'a new charge, and heard then for the first time'), he echoes the start of Cicero's defence of Ligarius ('A new charge, and not heard before this day'); and when Caecina Severus and Valerius Messalinus lead a senatorial debate on governors' wives (3.33–4), the debate re-enacts that presented by Livy (34.2–7) between Cato the Censor and L. Valerius in 195 B.C. on the status of women.[54]

The juxtaposition of Tacitus' text with Livy's raises an important question. Tacitus reports the speeches of Caecina and Valerius at some length; but do these speeches derive from a record or transcript of the originals in the 'acts of the senate' (*acta senatus*), to which Tacitus has merely added Livian 'colouring', or did Tacitus dispense with originals, basing his speeches on a combination of his own invention (*inuentio*) and Livy's text? Syme firmly believed that Tacitus' excellence as a historian in the *Annals* is to be explained by his personal perusal of the senatorial archives;[55] others have held an opposite view with equal firmness.[56] Since the *acta* have not survived, the matter cannot be proved conclusively one way or the other, and it is difficult to know what to infer from the fact that Tacitus refers to the *acta* only once and in a late book (15.74.3).[57]

Let us, then, rephrase the above question. When is a source not a source? Augustus transmitted to posterity a record of his achievements which is known as the *Res Gestae*,[58] of which a copy has been preserved on the walls of a temple in Ancyra (modern Ankara). Near the beginning of the *Annals* positive and negative assessments of Augustus are ascribed by Tacitus to opposing groups of the dead emperor's contemporaries (1.9–10): Tacitus makes no reference to the *Res Gestae* to support the positive assessment but typically parodies the document in the negative.[59] Thus Augustus' famous opening reads as follows (1.1):

At the age of nineteen years, on my personal [*priuato*] initiative and at personal [*priuata*] expense, I collected together [*comparaui*] an army [*exercitum*] with which I redeemed the freedom of the republic, oppressed by the domination [*dominatione*] of a faction.

This claim is transmuted by Tacitus as follows (1.10.1):

In a desire for dominion [*dominandi*] . . . an army [*exercitum*] had been collected [*paratum*] by a youth in a personal capacity [*priuato*].

Instead of a proud reference to tender years, Tacitus has used the potentially derogatory 'youth' (*adulescente*);[60] instead of Augustus' personal initiative, Tacitus has underlined his lack of official status (*priuato*); and instead of Augustus' freeing the state from domination, Tacitus has made domination his motive for acting. This transmutation suggests that Tacitus was using the *Res Gestae*, not as a 'source' (the facts will in any case have been well known), but as an inviting text whose official line he could subject to malicious reinterpretation.

A speech of the emperor Claudius has been partly preserved on bronze at Lyons in France, and a comparison of Tacitus' version at *Annals* 11.24 shows that he was familiar with it.[61] One of the most interesting features of the texts is that, while Tacitus is referring to Claudius' speech, Claudius himself refers to the speech of Canuleius at Livy 4.3.2–5.6.[62] That Tacitus knew of the emperor's reference is not certain but very likely, since Tacitus opens his version of Claudius' speech with these words (11.24.1):

Maiores mei, quorum antiquissimus Clausus origine Sabina simul in ciuitatem Romanam et in familias patriciorum adscitus est, . . .

My ancestors, of whom the most ancient, Clausus, of Sabine origin, was adopted simultaneously into Roman citizenship and into the families of the patricians, . . .

There is no analogue to these words in the extant portions of Claudius' own text; and, although it is obviously possible that Tacitus derived them from a non-extant part, it is tempting to speculate that he derived them directly from Livy (4.3.14):

non *in ciuitatem* modo . . . sed etiam *in patriciorum* numerum . . .

not only into citizenship . . . but also into the class of patricians . . .

With the change of *non . . . modo . . . sed etiam* to *simul . . . et*, Tacitus has opened his version with a reference to the very text to which Claudius himself was alluding. In this case, while Claudius' speech no doubt provided Tacitus with useful material for his account of A.D. 48, his 'window reference' to Livy is so typical of learned Latin poetry that his instincts in using the emperor's speech seem as much literary as (in our terms) historical.[63]

Until very recently the Claudian speech and Tacitus' version thereof constituted the only case where an original document could be compared directly with Tacitus' text. But the startling discovery of new inscriptions in Spain has transformed the scale of our evidence almost overnight. The so-called *Tabula Siarensis* records decisions taken by the senate late in A.D. 19 to honour Germanicus on his death. The last few lines of the inscription overlap with the first few lines of the *Tabula Hebana*, which has been known to scholars for fifty years;[64] but the bulk of the new inscription was unknown before its publication in 1984 and was thus unavailable to the two modern commentators on *Annals* 2, chapters 82–4 of which deal with the aftermath of Germanicus' death.[65]

Even more remarkable, however, is the discovery in Spain of a copy of 'the senate's decree on the elder Piso', which resulted from the trial of Cn. Calpurnius Piso for treason in A.D. 20.[66] Tacitus' account of the trial is found early in *Annals* 3 (7–19) and, like his account of the relationship between Piso and Germanicus in *Annals* 2 (55–8, 69–81), may be compared with the official version of events which the inscription records.[67] There are numerous similarities between Tacitus and the inscription, perhaps the most interesting being that between the endings of the two texts: the decree ends by recording that the senate had decided on the widest possible publication for it 'so that the stages of the conduct of the whole case could more easily be transmitted to the memory of posterity' (lines 165–6); Tacitus ends by saying that the ambiguities surrounding Germanicus' death have not been dispelled by time, 'in as much as some people hold every kind of hearsay as confirmed, others turn truth into its converse, and each swells with posterity' (19.2). The contexts of, and references to, posterity seem to amount to more than mere coincidence: it appears likely that Tacitus has re-cast the words of the decree to make an entirely different (and almost opposite) point. The procedure is typical of the way in which Tacitus has surrounded his narrative of the trial with rumour and hearsay which contradict the assured assertiveness of the official document.

The most obvious example of this difference is in the matter of Piso's death. The senatorial decree not only takes it for granted that Piso committed suicide but also interprets the suicide as an admission of guilt (6–7 'whether he seemed rightly to have taken his own life', 18–19 'although . . . he had exacted punishment from himself'); Tacitus, though he too implies (but does not go so far as to state) that Piso committed suicide (3.15.3), inserts into his narrative an extended parenthesis in which he records a rumour that Piso was murdered (3.16.1). And, though the author himself declines to give his assent to the rumour, he nevertheless goes out of his way to present it as authoritatively as possible.[68] Tacitus thus makes a major contribution to the ambiguity of the tradition to which he draws attention at the end of his account.[69]

The most absorbing problem raised by the discovery of the Pisonian inscription is that of the date of Piso's trial. During his narrative of the trial Tacitus twice alludes (3.11.1, 19.3) to an ovation for Tiberius' son, Drusus, which is dated by the official calendars (*fasti*) to 28 May A.D. 20.[70] After the second of these allusions Tacitus describes warfare in Africa (3.20–1), which presumably took place during the summer months, and the war in turn is followed by the account of a trial which may be datable to September (3.22–3).[71] In other words, Tacitus' narrative seems to follow a chronological sequence, beginning with

Piso's trial in the late spring. Yet the senatorial decree is dated 10 December A.D. 20 (lines 1–5, 175), from which a natural inference is that the trial itself took place, not in May (as scholars have assumed from Tacitus), but in November/December.

If the trial did indeed take place towards the very end of the year, some generally held and basic assumptions about Tacitean narrative require overhauling: Tacitus is evidently quite capable of putting into the first half of a narrative year an event of signal importance which took place in the second half of an actual year.[72] Such an overhaul is, however, a problem for those scholars who believe that Tacitus' annalistic scheme 'orders events . . . as they occur'.[73] Such scholars will therefore be compelled to believe that the inscription does not record the trial of Piso itself but, for example, a later meeting of the senate which took place more than six months afterwards in order to reassert decisions taken at the trial in May.[74]

The importance of Piso's trial no doubt ensured that its outline was familiar to Tacitus' contemporaries and that some of its details were recorded by at least one of his (now lost) predecessors; but the similarities between his account and the inscription strongly suggest that he enjoyed access to a copy of the senatorial decree (or of something very like it) in the same way as he did in the case of Claudius' speech (above, p. 00). We should nevertheless be cautious about assuming that Tacitus found his evidence by searching the *acta senatus* (above, p. 98): our knowledge of Roman archival practice suggests that 'in the management of public documentation, deposition – and, for important texts, display – was of much greater importance than retrieval'.[75] Tacitus' older contemporary, Josephus, talks of ancient Roman decrees which are 'fixed up in public places of the cities and are still inscribed on bronze tablets on the Capitol' (*Ant. Jud.* 14.188), while a more exact contemporary, Suetonius, says that, since three thousand bronze tablets had been destroyed in the conflagration of the Capitol, Vespasian undertook to restore this 'most fine and ancient evidence of empire, in which were included senatorial decrees almost from the start of the City' (*Vesp.* 8.5, cf. Tac. *H.* 4.40.2). Rome in the early empire was evidently a city overlaid with a mass of officially inspired information, to which its literate inhabitants had potential access. It is to be inferred from the Pisonian inscription itself (lines 169–70) that a bronze copy of it will have been displayed permanently and publicly in a prominent position at Rome:[76] all that was needed to transform such a text into history was literary skill and a preoccupation with the past.

The Pisonian inscription and Claudius' speech evidently represent only an infinitesimal fraction of the documentation on display in imperial Rome.[77] It is therefore inevitable that in the vast majority of cases we can know neither whether whether Tacitus is relying on such material or on some lost predecessor nor the extent to which he has resorted to the intertextual invention so familiar from earlier historiography.

When Pliny wrote to Tacitus volunteering details of his personal involvement in an episode in A.D. 93, so that his friend could include the episode in his *Histories* (above, p. 88), he ended his letter with these remarks (*Ep.* 7.33.10):[78]

These things, no matter what they are like, you will make more famous, more illustrious, and greater, although I do not demand that you exceed the limit of the case as conducted: for history ought not to transcend the truth, and truth is adequate for honourable actions.

Such remarks prompt the question of how the historian was supposed to produce a narrative which would live up to the expectations of his eager correspondent. Pliny assumes that the existence of the episode and perhaps also its outline will be known to Tacitus, 'since it appears in the public record' (*Ep.* 7.33.3);[79] and Pliny himself supplied Tacitus with all the extra information he needed to know (for otherwise Pliny would have written at greater length): what input was Pliny expecting from Tacitus to justify the comparative 'greater' (*maiora*)?

It is possible, but of course unprovable, that Pliny was hoping for the extra dimension provided by allusion, whereby Tacitus would describe the episode in terms of some famous forerunner: indeed, when Pliny reports to Tacitus that his action had been commended by the emperor Nerva as 'like that of the ancients' (*Ep.* 7.33.9), he may have been nudging his friend in this direction. Since the relevant part of the *Histories* has not survived, we cannot tell whether Tacitus took up the hint; but successive passages of *Annals* 14 will show what Pliny may have had in mind. The debate at 14.42–5 recalls the famous debate at the end of Sallust's *Bellum Catilinae* (51–2: above, p. 19), while that at 14.48–9 recalls the case of Clutorius Priscus in *Annals* 3 (49–51), which in its turn also recalls the same Sallustian 'original'.[80] Such intertextuality provided not only verisimilar material to fill out an episode but also, in the case of a famous debate such as Sallust's, extra resonances of contrast and comparison for those readers whose acquaintance with Sallust's text was as intimate as that of Tacitus himself.[81]

Tiberius

Tacitus' account of Tiberius' principate (A.D. 14–37) is commonly acknowledged to be his masterpiece: it occupies the first six books of the *Annals* and survives in a more complete form than any other narrative unit of comparable length. Many readers believe themselves familiar with the Tacitean Tiberius: he dominates the narrative which is devoted to him; often episodes are so structured as to conclude climactically with his intervention in, or reaction to, events; his presence is so pervasive that verbs without an expressed subject, or otherwise unexplained references to 'he' or 'him', are taken for granted as alluding to the *princeps*; and, though he is a consistent victim of Tacitean innuendo,[82] the slant of the narrative is often at odds with the 'facts' which that narrative conveys.[83] Tacitus was at once seduced and repelled by a fascinating personality.[84] Yet this is by no means the whole story.

As we have seen (p. 91), the start of the main Tiberian narrative (1.6) is separated from the *Annals'* preface (1.1) by two short sections on the career and last days of Augustus (1.2.1–4.1 and 1.4.2–5.4). During this interlude Tacitus reports contemporary opinion on Augustus' potential successors, Agrippa Postumus and Tiberius himself, of whom the latter receives a character sketch in reported speech (1.4.3–5): his name is followed by references to his family, infancy, youth, honours, and habits.[85] The sketch ends as follows:

In addition there was his mother, with her woman's unruliness: enslavement to her – a female – would be compulsory, and to two juveniles as well, who for a while would oppress the state and at some time tear it apart.

Though commentators tend to remark on the commonplace notions of female domination and sibling rivalry, they slide over Tiberius' envisaged subservience to his sons, Germanicus and Drusus. Yet this slur discloses a key element of Tiberius' presentation.[86]

The Tiberian hexad closes with an obituary notice of the *princeps* (6.51). Its first paragraph (1–2) falls into five parts, four of which concentrate on the man's earlier life, and in its wording (e.g. a reference to 'his earliest infancy') it seems designed to recall the introductory sketch (mentioned above). The second paragraph (3) divides Tiberius' behaviour (*mores*) into five phases, four of which are accounted for by his twenty-three years as emperor:

In his behaviour too there were differing phases: one exceptional in life and reputation as long as he was a private individual or in commands under Augustus; secretive and guileful at representing virtues while Germanicus and Drusus survived; the man was likewise a blend of good and evil during his mother's preservation; infamous for savagery, but with his lusts concealed, while he loved Sejanus or feared him; lastly he erupted into crimes and degradations alike when at last, with the removal of shame and dread, *suo tantum ingenio utebatur*.

From this paragraph scholars have drawn three influential conclusions: (a) Tacitus resembles other ancient writers in believing that a person's character (*ingenium*) was fixed at birth and could not change; (b) Tiberius' *ingenium* was innately evil, but this was revealed only during the final phase of his life, since in the previous phases he was restrained by the individuals named; (c) his restraint took the form of pretending virtues and hiding vices, which explains why such features as simulation (*simulatio*) and dissimulation (*dissimulatio*) are attributed to him frequently in the main narrative.[87]

Though these conclusions are repeated in all the standard works, there are serious objections to be brought against each in turn: (a) Tacitus elsewhere (6.48.2, *H.* 1.50.4) expresses the view that a person's character could change, a view which recently has been shown to be not uncommon amongst other ancient writers;[88] (b) though Livia is elsewhere described as a restraining influence (5.3.1), Tacitus in his main narrative describes Sejanus as the opposite, namely a stimulating influence (4.1.1); (c) dissimulation continues to be practised by Tiberius even up to the last moments of his life (6.50.1), when, according to the hypothesis, all need for such deception should long since have passed.[89] Evidently the obituary notice requires a different interpretation.[90]

The last four phases, which are coextensive with the period covered by Tacitus' Tiberian narrative, are separated from one another by the deaths of prominent individuals; but the first of these phases is unusual in that it is identified by two deaths, between which there intervene four years and a whole book of the *Annals*: Germanicus died in A.D. 19 (2.72.2), Drusus in A.D. 23 (4.8.1–2). In the present case, and in contrast to the introductory sketch, scholars do indeed remark on the seemingly odd combination of Germanicus and Drusus, but only to express their bafflement at its relevance; yet the thread linking Germanicus and Drusus both to each other and to Livia and Sejanus is that all four of them were helpers or partners of Tiberius. It is this relationship, attested by other authors,[91] which is disparagingly described as 'compulsory enslavement' (*seruiendum*) in the introductory sketch.[92] Though the description is a slur, 'enslavement' alludes to the essential truth that

Tiberius was dependent upon others. As each of this partners died, he was left increasingly isolated, until, with the death of Sejanus, 'he had only himself to rely on' (*suo tantum ingenio utebatur*).[93] And, since his increasing isolation was accompanied by a progressive deterioration in his behaviour, the extent of his reliance on the named individuals is emphasized. Thus the introductory sketch and the obituary notice complement and explain each other: although Tiberius undeniably dominates the main narrative, the hexad is framed by passages which, somewhat paradoxically, present the emperor as a dependent personality.

This dependence is established by the very first episode of the Tiberian narrative, the murder of Agrippa Postumus, Tiberius' only rival for the succession (1.6).[94] In a programmatic series of brilliant manoeuvres, Tacitus as first seems to imply that Tiberius had instigated the murder but was allowing the dead Augustus to take the blame (1.6.1); but then, having demonstrated the unlikelihood of Augustus' involvement, Tacitus records the contemporary belief that Tiberius and Livia were jointly responsible (1.6.2). This belief seems borne out by the executioner himself, who reported to Tiberius that his command had been carried out; yet Tiberius not only denied having issued a command but said that an account of the matter should be given in the senate (1.6.3), whereupon Sallustius Crispus, a friend of Augustus, appealed to Livia to prevent Tiberius from publicizing the scandal in the senate: the condition of being *imperator* ('Commander') was that the account would balance only if it were rendered to a single individual (*uni*). It is not until the last stages of the episode that it becomes clear that Sallustius and Livia between them have arranged Postumus' death without Tiberius' knowledge: not only was the ruler of the world ignorant of the first act carried out in his name by his mother and an assistant of his father's but he is dependent on the experienced Sallustius both for extricating him from the crisis and for his first lesson in how to be *imperator* or *princeps*. And that lesson could scarcely have been less welcome: whereas Tiberius' instinctive reaction to the crisis had been to share the problem with the senate, Sallustius warned him that from now on he was on his own.

This picture is developed further in Tacitus' brilliant description of the second meeting of the senate at the start of Tiberius' reign (1.10.8–13.6). Tiberius began by saying that, whereas Augustus' intellect meant that he had been capable of running the empire single-handedly (1.11.1 '*solam . . .* mentem'), he himself did not want exclusive responsibility ('non ad *unum* omnia deferrent') but hoped for a partnership of

distinguished men (*'sociatis* laboribus'). But the senate protested vigor-
ously, whereupon the *princeps*, in a dramatic gesture, ordered Augustus'
own account of the extent of the empire to be produced and read out
(1.11.3–4). Tiberius no doubt imagined that this evidence would
support his case; and he also said that, though unequal to the whole
task, he himself would accept whatever part was given to him (1.12.1).
But, when Asinius Gallus then asked him what part he wanted, Tiberius
after an initial silence replied that it was inconsistent with his diffidence
to choose or avoid any specific element, although he would prefer to be
excused the burden altogether (1.12.2). At this, Gallus explained that
the point of his question had been to elicit from Tiberius himself an
acknowledgement that the empire needed to be ruled by the mind of a
single individual (1.12.3 *'unius* animo'), a public recognition of the
warning which Sallustius had impressed upon the *princeps* earlier in
private. Various other prominent members made interventions similar
to that of Gallus (1.13.1, 4), whereupon Tiberius, exhausted by all the
wrangling, took refuge in an evasive silence: he did not say that he was
assuming command of the empire, but at the same time he withdrew
from repeatedly denying what the senators repeatedly requested
(1.13.5). This characteristically Tiberian evasion is of crucial importance, since, while appearing to have acceded to the senate's requests,
without further ado he proceeded to put into practice the proposal
which he himself had made: as we have already seen (above, p. 104), he
effectively made Germanicus and Drusus his joint partners in affairs.

Though Germanicus died in A.D. 19, Tiberius seemed to be realizing
his ultimate ambition in A.D. 21, when, partnered by his son Drusus in
the consulship, he withdrew from Rome to Campania (3.31.2):

gradually considering a long and continuous absence, or so that Drusus, with his father
removed, might fulfil the responsibilities of the consulship on his own.

The *princeps* was still absent in the following year, when he requested the
tribunician power for his son and designated him officially as his
'partner in toil' (3.56.4 *laboris participem*). Tiberius thereby seemed to
have achieved his twin goals of partnership and withdrawal which he
had expressed several years earlier,[95] but this desired state of affairs was
not to last long, since he was soon brought back to the city by news of an
illness of his mother's (3.64.1). And in the following year Drusus died,
an event which, according to Tacitus' obituary notice for the emperor,
marked the end of the first phase of the reign.

Although the obituary notice implicitly designates Germanicus as no less an assistant of Tiberius than was Drusus, in the main narrative this role has to be inferred from the regularity with which he is mentioned alongside Drusus (see esp. 1.14.3, 1.52.1–3, 2.43.1 and 5–6, 2.64.1, 2.84.2, 3.56.3).[96] The explanation for this treatment is twofold. On the one hand Tacitus is pursuing a rather different agenda in the case of Germanicus, whom he uses as a foil for Tiberius.[97] On the other hand it is clear from the obituary notice that Tacitus was interested in how Tiberius was affected when the death of his various partners deprived him of assistance; and, since Germanicus' and Drusus' was a joint partnership during the former's lifetime, the question of Tiberius' deprivation did not become a possibility until Germanicus' death in A.D. 19 left only one of the *princeps*' sons remaining alive.[98]

It was nevertheless perhaps as a result of Germanicus' death that Tiberius started to rely also on Sejanus and to call him his 'ally in toil' (*socium laborum*). Tacitus associates this title with the year A.D. 20, the year after Germanicus' death, but delays his recording of it until his narrative of A.D. 23 is under way in Book 4 (2.3).[99] The reason for this delay is that Tacitus is making the structure of his narrative conform to the schematization of the obituary notice. In the latter the first phase of Tiberius' principate is separated from the second by Drusus' death, and this separation is marked in the narrative by the division of the hexad into two at the year 23 and by the description of that year as a turning-point at the start of Book 4 (1.1, 6.1, 7.1).[100] Any earlier allusion to Sejanus' role would have detracted from this dramatic structural division. Tacitus then capitalizes on this narrative delay by making Sejanus' role as Tiberius' helper the motivating factor behind Drusus' death, which in turn precipitates the action of Book 4. For Drusus, as the *princeps*' son, naturally resented the favouritism now bestowed on a non-familial rival (4.7.1):

frequently complaining that, with a son alive and well, another was being called assistant in command [*adiutorem imperii*]; and how short the remaining stage until he was spoken of as colleague!

And it was this resentment which persuaded Sejanus in A.D. 23 to make a preemptive strike against Drusus, whom he poisoned in such a way as to make his death seem like a fatal illness (4.8.1).

With Drusus' death the field was left clearer for Sejanus.[101] Having attempted to persuade Tiberius to withdraw from Rome (4.41), he saw his wishes fulfilled in A.D. 26, when Tiberius withdrew a second time to Campania (4.57.1) and thence to Capri in the following year (4.67.1).

The circumstances of A.D. 21–2 were thereby resurrected, except that this time Tiberius was never to return to the city (cf. 4.58.2–3, 6.15.3). One of the considerations which allegedly convinced Tiberius to withdraw was the influence of his mother (4.57.3 'forced out by his mother's unruliness'), of which evidence has been provided at strategic points in the earlier narrative (e.g. 1.13.6, 3.15.1, 3.17.1–2, 3.64.2).[102] Now in A.D. 26 Tacitus aptly sums up the relationship between mother and son as a partnership which Tiberius despised but could not bring himself to abandon (4.57.3 *dominationis sociam aspernabatur neque depellere poterat*). Whether this inability was due to her dominance or his own dependency is left unsaid; but in any case she died three years later, her death being placed prominently by Tacitus at the very start of Book 5 (1.1).

According to Tiberius' obituary notice Livia's death marked the end of the second phase of Tiberius' principate, and in the main narrative Tacitus describes the effects of her death as follows (5.3.1):

Thenceforwards it was sheer, overhanging despotism [*praerupta et urgens dominatio*]. For, with Augusta safe and sound, there had still been a refuge, because Tiberius' deference to his mother was deep-rooted, nor did Sejanus dare to outstrip her parent's authority; but then, as if released from harness [*uelut frenis exsoluti*], they charged ahead [*proruperunt*].

praerupta indicates that the joint domination of Tiberius and Sejanus is seen as a dangerous cliff, an image which *urgens* sustains.[103] But soon the image changes and the two malefactors are envisaged as animals released from harness before they charge forwards.[104] Unfortunately our text of the *Annals* breaks off shortly after this passage and we are deprived of Tacitus' account of Sejanus' downfall and hence of the momentous event which separated the penultimate from the final phase of Tiberius' principate. But we are told by Suetonius that, when Tiberius wrote to denounce Sejanus to the senate, he described himself as now 'an old man and alone' (*Tib.* 65.1 *senem et solum*). The emperor thus spent the last years of his principate in the isolation which he had deplored at the start of it, a bitter parody of the loneliness of command with which he was urged by Sallustius Crispus and Asinius Gallus to come to terms; his only consolation was that he had also achieved the withdrawal from affairs which his successive attempts at partnership had been designed to promote.

This is a rather different Tiberius from the one-dimensional portrait of a manipulative autocrat which is to be found in many history books and other modern accounts. Tiberius had a highly developed sense of responsibility to the state, but, as the first paragraph of his obituary notice makes clear, in the years before A.D. 14 he had been victimized too often not to be affected in the years of his principate. Tacitus has made Tiberius' dependency upon others the single factor which regulates his career as a whole and defines the periods within it. The second paragraph of his obituary notice explains, retrospectively as it were, the nuances and contradictions of behaviour in this most memorably narrated of antiquity's tyrants.

Variations

It is an axiom of scholarship that in Tacitus' opinion the chief function of history is to ensure that virtues are recorded and that posterity is deterred from evil by reading about examples of evil behaviour.[105] This view, which is said to be supported by similar statements in Sallust (*BJ* 4.1, 5–6) and Livy (*Praef.* 10), is based on the conventional punctuation of a famous passage in *Annals* 3 (65.1).[106] Now passages often become famous because they are taken out of context; and, having become famous, they take on a life of their own and are rarely questioned. Yet not only do Sallust and Livy say something significantly different from what is imputed to Tacitus[107] but Tacitus' passage, if re-punctuated, may itself be interpreted differently:

exsequi sententias haud institui nisi insignes per honestum aut notabili dedecore (quod praecipuum munus annalium reor), ne uirtutes sileantur utque prauis dictis factisque ex posteritate et infamia metus sit.

It has not been my practice to go through senatorial motions in detail except those conspicuous for honour or of notable shame (which I reckon to be a very great responsibility of annals), lest virtues be silenced and so that crooked words and deeds should, in the light of posterity and infamy, attract dread.

On this interpretation Tacitus is not defining the chief function of history at all: he is apologizing for the monotonous subject-matter of the year being narrated (A.D. 22) and is reassuring his readers that, well aware of the historian's duty to be selective,[108] he has described only events which are conspicuously honourable and notably shameful (he refers to the senatorial debates at 3.60–3 and 56–9 respectively).[109] Likewise in the famous digression in *Annals* 4 Tacitus apologizes for describing matters that seem 'perhaps trivial and insignificant to relate' (32.1) and expresses his awareness that readers

expect variety (33.3). Such personal interventions (which reappear in
various forms at *A.* 6.7.5, 13.31.1, 14.64.3, 16.16.1–2) are designed
both to enhance his authorial status and to underline the nature of
the material with which he is obliged to deal. When Pliny replied to
Tacitus with details of the eruption of Vesuvius (above, p. 88), he
knew that his friend would treat them selectively (*Ep.* 6.16.22 'you
will select the most important elements') and he admitted, no doubt
disingenuously, that some of them were 'not worthy of history' (*Ep.*
6.20.20).

The reader's desire for variety is brilliantly accommodated by *Annals*
15. The first thirty-two chapters of the book embrace the continuation
of A.D. 62 (1–22) and the whole of A.D. 63 (23–32): although there are
brief domestic interludes (18–23, 32), the bulk of the narrative is
devoted to exploits in the east. Foreign affairs conventionally offered
the change to an exotic locality and the chance of enthralling adventures
(cf. *A.* 4.33.3);[110] and the understated opening of the book (above, p. 94
n. 36) is merely the prelude to the incompetence of Caesennius Paetus,
which is seen in terms of the débâcle at the Caudine Forks in 321 B.C.,
and its dramatic reversal by Corbulo, his commander in chief.[111] With
the advent of the following year, however, Tacitus turns to domestic
affairs and adopts the mode of the paradoxographer in order to express
the bizarre truths that Rome exhibits the characteristics of the alien city
of Alexandria and that Nero's behaviour is the reverse of everything
Roman (37).[112] This passage is immediately followed by the famous
description of the fire of Rome (38–41): while Rome burned, Nero
sang, himself now transforming the capital of the empire into the ancient
city of Troy (39.3 'he had taken to his domestic stage and sung of the
Trojan destruction, comparing present evils to ancient disasters'). Nero
thereby turned back Roman history to its very beginning so that he
could restart it under the capital's new name of Neropolis (Suet. *Nero*
55). The narrative of the following year is entirely taken up (until the
end of the book) with the conspiracy of Piso (48–74), which Tacitus,
changing his authorial mode yet again, treats like a play: the protagonists, as if mesmerized by the fantasy world inhabited and encouraged
by the 'stage-struck commander', themselves behave like actors and,
losing all contact with reality, forfeit the success of the conspiracy.[113]

Annals 15 represents a dazzling sequence of varied narrative modes,
but it is well known that Tacitus' obsession with variety extends also to
style and language. The most obvious illustration is his constant refusal
to balance constructions: coordination or disjunction is used to juxta-

pose clauses of different types (e.g. causal and purpose at *H.* 3.4.2 *non quia industria Flauiani egebat sed ut consulare nomen surgentibus cum maxime partibus honesta specie praetenderetur*) or clauses and phrases (e.g. causal ablative and negative purpose at *H.* 1.7.2 *mobilitate ingenii an ne altius scrutaretur*). Examples and types could be extended almost indefinitely.[114] Similarly Tacitus ends sentences later than one would expect: no sooner does the end seem nigh than he will add an appendage (often an ablative absolute), deadly or savage in its comment (e.g. *A.* 13.17.1 *nox eadem necem Britannici et rogum coniunxit, prouiso ante funebri paratu, qui modicus fuit,* 'a single night saw Germanicus' execution and pyre – earlier provision having been made for his funeral trappings, which were modest').[115] Innovative or unusual syntax, such as his use of the genitive gerundive of purpose (e.g. *A.* 2.59.1 *Germanicus Aegyptum proficiscitur cognoscendae antiquitatis*), jostles with archaizing, rare, or obsolete vocabulary.[116] He avoids, varies, or 'misuses' technical terms,[117] will not call a spade a spade (*A.* 1.65.7), and an encounter with Asinius Gallus in one place (*A.* 1.12.2) almost guarantees that our next encounter will be with Gallus Asinius (*A.* 1.13.2).[118] The cumulative effect is discordant and bizarre, as if reflecting essential truths about the world which Tacitus presents to his readers.

Some readers, however, are likely to attribute to Tacitus an almost wilful perversity. Here, at any rate, is what Napoleon said to the poet Wieland in 1808:[119]

'What an involved style! How obscure! I am not a great Latin scholar, but Tacitus' obscurity displays itself in ten or twelve Italian and French translations that I have read. I, therefore, conclude that his chief *quality* is obscurity, that it springs from that which one calls his genius, as well as from his style, and that it is so connected with his manner of expressing himself only because it is in his conception. . . . Am I not right, *Monsieur Wieland*? But I am interrupting you. We are not here to speak of Tacitus. Look! How well the Czar Alexander dances!'

It is therefore a paradox that Tacitus peppers his pages with words suggesting pretence and masquerade (*species, facies, imago, simulacrum*),[120] as if to imply he has disclosed and penetrated the façade which is the defining feature of the Roman principate. Indeed it was his perceived penetration which attracted Gibbon.[121] But, if the writing of history 'is to a great extent a process of penetrating disguise and uncovering what is hidden', there is always the danger to which Macaulay was susceptible: 'in rejecting the accepted and traditional, the great temptation was to reverse them, to adopt habitually a posture of contrariness'.[122] The posture was not unknown to Tacitus, who in his monograph on oratory says of the character Aper that 'he does not even think that himself but . . . has taken on the role of saying the opposite' (*Dialogus* 24.2).[123]

Macaulay too 'disliked the laudatory mode': when he heard praise and general admiration for someone, 'it always spurred him on to find something to be blamed'.[124] Likewise Mary Gladstone objected to Lord Acton: 'There is in some quarter a general idea that you do nothing but criticise with folded hands – that you are always negative – that nobody knows anything at all about your real opinions – that you continually pull down and tear to pieces, without raising up or edifying'.[125] Yet Macaulay told 'a tale which had an uplifting moral and a happy ending' and his 'steadily advancing prose reflects his theme of advance and success after setbacks and disasters', whereas for Acton 'history was an iconoclast'.[126] In this respect Tacitus was nearer to Acton than to Macaulay, yet, while Acton is widely assumed to have written almost nothing, it is Macaulay and Tacitus whose works live on.

Tacitus' sustained indictment of a society in decline is of a piece with his suggestively diplomatic silence about Trajan; yet there is a passage in the *Annals* where he goes out of his way to praise the Trajanic age as rivalling past excellence and as providing an example for posterity to imitate (3.55.5):[127]

Nor was everything better in the time of our forebears, but our age too has produced many instances of artistic excellence to be imitated by posterity. However that may be,[128] may these contests of ours with our ancestors endure honourably.

Sir Ronald Syme believed that Tacitus is here referring to Trajanic literature, including, therefore, the *Histories* and *Annals* themselves.[129] If that is so, Tacitus knew well enough that he had chosen the right subjects for treatment and had found the right style with which to treat them. Pliny was quite justified (above, p. 88) in having such confidence in the immortality of his friend's work.

NOTES

1. For the dating of Pliny's letters see A. N. Sherwin-White, *The Letters of Pliny* (Oxford, 1966), 36–8.

2. The preface is of course an integral part of his book or 'work' (*opus*), on the various nuances of which Tacitus is evidently playing.

3. The details of Tacitus' early career are not quite certain, but it is known that he was praetor in A.D. 88, suffect consul in 97 and proconsul of Asia in 112/13. It has recently been suggested by G. Alföldy (*MDAI(R)* 102 (1995), 251–68) that a fragmentary funerary inscription

from Rome (*CIL* 6.1574) is that of Tacitus: if so, he had had the distinction of being *quaestor Augusti*.

4. i.e. though the contemporary period may be 'more productive', his chosen period nevertheless has its own variety of 'richness'. The transmitted *opimum* has often been questioned (e.g. by Syme in *RP*, 6.205–8), and Wellesley in his edition re-writes the opening of the sentence entirely (*Tempus adgredior dirum casibus*); but the metaphorical context (continued at 1.3.1 *sterile*) suggests that the word is correct.

5. See *RICH*, 165–7.

6. The standard work on the theme of civil war in Latin literature is P. Jal, *La Guerre civile à Rome* (Paris, 1963).

7. Of which Tacitus' work is very full: see Plass (1988), who is principally concerned with the political and other effects of wit. Yet many of Tacitus' examples seem to have no particular purpose: see e.g. *H.* 2.22.3 *Caecinae haud alienus* (Caecina's cognomen was Alienus) or *A.* 1.13.6 *Tiberius casu an manibus eius impeditus prociderat* (where *casu* is from the same root as *prociderat*, *manibus* interacts with the *pes* root of *impeditus*, and knees [*genua*] are mentioned earlier in the sentence).

8. For a survey of opinion see Syme (1958), 145 n. 5.

9. Syme (1958), 145.

10. For a recent discussion see T. Cole, *YCS* 29 (1992), 231–45. (The volume is devoted to 'Beginnings in classical literature'.)

11. Syme (1939), 507.

12. See A. D. Leeman, 'Structure and meaning in the prologues of Tacitus', *YCS* 23 (1973), 169–208 (at 188–9). Remarkably few scholars seem to have recognized Tacitus' clear procedure.

13. E.g. Syme (1958), 367–71, 427, *RP* 3.939–40, 1027–8. For a recent discussion of the whole matter see M. Griffin, 'Tacitus, Tiberius and the principate', in *Leaders and Masses in the Roman World* (ed. I. Malkin & Z. W. Rubinsohn, Leiden, 1995), esp. 33–43.

14. We also lack most of *A.* 5, all of *A.* 7–10, and some of *A.* 11.

15. *Comm. Zach.* 3.14 'in thirty volumes he wrote down the lives of the Caesars after Augustus up to the death of Domitian'.

16. See pp. 183–4 of Wellesley's edition of the *Histories*, where he also argues the likelihood that *Historiae* was the original title of the *Histories*. See also Goodyear (1972), 85–7 and, for a fascinating study of the titulature of ancient books, Horsfall (1981).

17. For the textual transmission of Tacitus' works see L. D. Reynolds (ed.), *Texts and Transmission* (Oxford, 1983), 406–11.

18. Goodyear (1970), 17–18.

19. See Syme (1958), 686–7.

20. R. H. Martin, 'Tacitus and the death of Augustus', *CQ* 5 (1955), 123–8.

21. On the other hand, if Tacitus died before completing the *Annals*, it would follow from St Jerome that the *Histories* comprised fourteen books; yet the clear break after *H.* 3 (see p. 96) perhaps suggests that a hexadic structure operated there too, in which case a total of fourteen books would be impossible.

22. It should be borne in mind that 'the promise of future work(s)' was a familiar literary motif (Woodman (1975), 287–8).

23. The contrast between Trajan and Domitian forms a major theme of Plin. *Pan.* (2–3, 53); likewise Velleius had greeted both Augustus' principate by contrasting it with the previous age (89.2–6) and Tiberius' principate by contrasting it with Augustus' (126.2–5). It is virtually certain that long before Trajan's time such contrasts had become standard as a method of praising the current ruler (cf. Plin. *Ep.* 3.13.2, 6.27.3). Tacitus capitalizes on this convention by reversing it at the start of Tiberius' reign (*A.* 1.10.7 *comparatione deterrima*, 'a very base comparison'; cf. Suet. *Tib.* 21.2, Dio 56.45.3). Pliny's *Panegyric* and the issues it raises, many of them relevant to Tacitus also, are superbly discussed by S. Bartsch, *Actors in the Audience* (Cambridge, Ma./London, 1994), 148–87.

24. This would be analogous to what is called 'figured speech', for which see the evidence assembled by R. R. Dyer, 'Rhetoric and Intention in Cicero's *Pro Marcello*', *JRS* 80 (1990), 26–30.

25. Syme (1958), 470–4, 826 (index '*ANNALES*, contemporary relevance').

26. The famous saying of B. Croce: see R. G. Collingwood, *The Idea of History* (Oxford,

1946), 202, A. Marwick, *The Nature of History* (London/Basingstoke, ³1989), 291–2. The precise dates of the composition of the *Annals* are not known: for the suggestion that *A.* 4 belongs to A.D. 115 see Martin–Woodman (1997), 102–3 and n. 1 (*contra* G. W. Bowersock, 'The Greek–Nabataean bilingual inscription at Ruwwâfa, Saudi Arabia', in *Le Monde grec: Hommages à Claire Préaux* (ed. J. Bingen et al., Brussels, 1975), 518–20).

27. Attacking the dead was a proverbially pointless exercise (see e.g. Plin. *NH* pref. 31). S. M. Braund in her new commentary explains the apparent contradiction in terms of *persona* and as a variation on a traditional satiric motif (*Juvenal: Satires 1* (Cambridge 1996), 116–21).

28. E. Courtney, *A Commentary on the Satires of Juvenal* (London, 1980), 81; see also N. Rudd, *Themes in Roman Satire* (London, 1986), 70–81. Tacitus' work constantly suggests comparison with Juvenal, though their relationship awaits further study. See, however, Syme, *RP*, 3.1135–57.

29. This whole subject is interestingly illustrated by Phaedrus, a writer of fables and contemporary with Tiberius, when he defends himself and his genre in the prologue to his Book 3. He first says that the genre was devised by slaves, who, 'because they did not dare to say what they wished' (cf. Tac. *H.* 1.1.4: above, p. 89), gave vent to their critical feelings through the allegory of fable (33–7). He then apologizes if a reader, because of a bad conscience, identifies himself with the faults portrayed in the fables: it is not the author's intention to brand individuals (45–50).

30. On the digression see Martin–Woodman (1997), 169–76.

31. There is an excellent discussion of this episode by H. Cancik-Lindemaier and H. Cancik, *Der altsprachliche Unterricht* 29 (1986), 4.16–35.

32. For a useful survey of 'closure' (i.e. how works of literature, or sections thereof, end) see Fowler (1989).

33. See above, p. 62.

34. The standard and invaluable discussion of these matters in Ginsburg (1981), who treats only the Tiberian books. Her tabulation of the various types of narrative year (p. 54) perhaps requires some modification, but the point made in the text above remains true. The narrative structure of each of Tacitus' works is analysed in great detail by G. Wille, *Der Aufbau der Werke des Tacitus* (Amsterdam, 1983).

35. See Woodman–Martin (1996), 77-9 and 87–8. (Book 1 of the *Annals* is clearly a special case: see p. 91.)

36. It is *A.* 15 which begins prosaically, perhaps as a prelude to the subsequent reversal (see p. 110).

37. Note pp. 1574–5 of R. H. Martin, 'Structure and interpretation in the "Annals" of Tacitus', *ANRW* 2.33.2.1500–81 (1990), a most valuable introduction to the content and organization of the surviving books; on the later books note too C. J. Classen, 'Tacitus – historian between republic and principate', *Mnem.* 41 (1988), 104–14.

38. 'Do historians . . . have to possess a special metaphorical capacity, a plastic or tactile imagination that can detect shapes and configurations where others less gifted see only jumble and confusion? In what ways is the sort of imagery any great historian chooses integrally related to his personality and his general outlook on the world?' (Clive (1989), 200–1). On metaphor see further pp. 96 and 108.

39. Syme (1958), 531 and n. 1; in general see Pelling, *TTT*, 79–81.

40. See Woodman–Martin (1996), 11, 79, 96–7, 489–90.

41. Tacitus has placed Arminius' obituary anachronistically in order to achieve this link (n. 72 below). For the beginning and ending of *A.* 4 see Martin–Woodman (1997) 18 and 262. The ending of *A.* 5 and beginning of *A.* 6 have not survived; for the ending of the latter see pp. 103–5. On freedom and related concepts in Tacitus see e.g. M. Morford, 'How Tacitus defined liberty', *ANRW* 2.33.5.3420–50 (1991), and M. Vielberg, *Pflichten, Werte, Ideale: eine Untersuchung zu den Wertvorstellungen des Tacitus* (Stuttgart, 1987).

42. See Heubner (1972), 151; also E. Fraenkel, 'Rome and Greek culture', *Kleine Beiträge* (Rome, 1964), 2.594. There is a recent study of obituary notices by Pomeroy (1991), who discusses those of cities in Appendix 1 (pp. 255–7). For deaths in Tacitus see also G. O. Hutchinson, *Latin Literature from Seneca to Juvenal* (Oxford, 1993), 257–68; this book contains various sections on Tacitus (see esp. pp. 50–62).

43. L. Damrosch, *Fictions of Reality in the Age of Hume and Johnson* (Madison/London,

1989), 109, on the body analogy in Gibbon and others; note also J. Béranger, *Recherches sur l'aspect idéologique du principat* (Basel, 1953), 218ff., C. Nicolet, *Space, Geography and Politics in the Early Roman Empire* (Ann Arbor, 1991), 192 and n. 9, and, on the symbolism of decapitation, R. Ash, 'Severed Heads', in *Plutarch and his Intellectual World* (ed. J. Mossman, London/Swansea, 1997), 196–200.

44. See Kraus (1994a) and (1994), 83–8 respectively. On the significance of the City of Rome and its buildings etc. there is much of interest in Vasaly (1993), e.g. 26–39 (with refs. to Camillus' speech in Livy).

45. There is a study of Vitellius' death-scene in D. S. Levene, 'Pity, fear and the historical audience: Tacitus on the fall of Vitellius', *The Passions in Roman Thought and Literature* (ed. Braund & Gill, Cambridge, 1997).

46. F. Pollock & F. W. Maitland, *The History of English Law Before the Time of Edward I* (Cambridge, ²1898), 1.1.

47. 'Intertextuality' is a modish word, now about thirty years old, to denote the fact that there is a relationship between texts (for a bibliography on the subject see de Jong–Sullivan (1994), 284). The word has the advantage over more traditional terms, such as 'imitation' or 'allusion', in that it implies nothing about whether the relationship in any given case is intentional. Nevertheless in the following section, in which literary texts (such as that of Livy) and documentary texts (such as inscriptions) are deliberately discussed side by side, it is assumed that each case is in fact intentional on Tacitus' part.

48. The third passage (*diuersa omnium . . . ciuilium armorum facies*) perhaps recalls Lucan, the epic poet of the civil war, in both theme (Luc. 1.1 *Bella . . . plus quam ciuilia*) and language (9.789 *facies . . . diuersa*).

49. See Pelling, *TTT*, 69, referring to Syme (1958), 375.

50. E. Keitel, 'Principate and civil war in the *Annals* of Tacitus', *AJP* 105 (1984), 306–25 (at 325). Note esp. Sen. *Clem.* 1.1.1 for a similar theme.

51. See A. J. Woodman, 'Self-imitation and the substance of history', *Creative Imitation and Latin Literature* (ed. David West and Tony Woodman, Cambridge, 1979), 143–55. Also below, n. 81.

52. 'This extra-perception [afforded to a historian by his privileged position] allowed him to range backwards and forwards through time, alive to a mysterious unfolding destiny, which is given greater tragic significance by the literary device of anticipatory prolepsis' (Tulloch (1988), 111 on Lord Acton).

53. For an excellent discussion of the meaningfulness of such intertextual character portrayals see J. Griffin, 'The creation of characters in the *Aeneid*', *Latin Poets and Roman Life* (London, 1985), 183–97.

54. See J. Ginsburg, '*In maiores certamina*: past and present in the Annals', *TTT*, 88–96; also Woodman–Martin (1996), 283–306.

55. See *RP*, 4.207ff.

56. See e.g. A. Momigliano, *The Classical Foundations of Modern Historiography* (Berkeley/Los Angeles/Oxford, 1990), 110ff.

57. Some scholars have detected another reference at *A.* 2.88.1 (see e.g. Goodyear (1981), 446) but the text is uncertain and the possibility seems remote.

58. There is a helpful edition and translation by P. A. Brunt and J. M. Moore (Oxford, 1967 and often reissued). Good remarks in Galinsky (1996), 10–20, 42–54.

59. This seems to have been pointed out first by F. Haverfield, 'Four notes on Tacitus', *JRS* 2 (1912), 197–9.

60. For the tone of this word see Ogilvie (²1970) on Liv. 2.56.10.

61. This inscription (*CIL* 13.1668 = *ILS* 212) is conveniently available in E. M. Smallwood, *Documents Illustrating the Principates of Gaius, Claudius and Nero* (Oxford, 1967, repr. 1984), no. 369 and is translated in *Inscriptions of the Roman Empire A.D. 14–117* (LACTOR 8, 1971), no. 34 or B. Levick, *The Government of the Roman Empire: A Sourcebook* (London, 1985), no. 159. For comparisons of the inscription with Tacitus see e.g. K. Wellesley, *G&R* 1 (1954), 13–33, N. P. Miller, *RhM* 99 (1956), 304–15, M. T. Griffin, *CQ* 32 (1982), 404–18, 40 (1990), 482–501, von Albrecht (1989), 136–59 (who has translations of each version). Note also Brock (1995), 209–11.

62. D. M. Last and R. M. Ogilvie, *Latomus* 17 (1958), 476–87. For Claudius' connection

with Livy see Suet. *Claud.* 41.1 'in adolescence he set about writing history under the encouragement of Livy'.

63. A 'window reference' occurs when C, who is referring to B (who in turn is referring to A), himself refers to A in order to demonstrate his awareness of B's procedure and perhaps also to correct it: see Thomas (1986), 188–9. Traces of Claudius' speech reappear in earlier parts of the *Annals* (esp. 4.65): Syme (1958), 708–10 argued that Tacitus, even when writing about Tiberius, already knew of Claudius' speech; G. B. Townend argued that this was unlikely and suggested that Tacitus had used as intermediary the historian Aufidius Bassus, who, being a contemporary of Claudius, would have had reason to refer complimentarily to the emperor's speech in his own history of the Tiberian years ('Claudius and the digressions in Tacitus', *RhM* 105 (1962), 364–5).

64. EJ, no. 94a, Sherk (1988), pp. 67–71.

65. The inscription was published by J. González, *ZPE* 55 (1984), 55–100, and is translated in Sherk (1988), no. 36 (pp. 63–7). The two commentators are Koestermann (1963) and Goodyear (1981).

66. See W. Eck, A. Caballos and F. Fernández, *Das Senatus Consultum de Cn. Pisone Patre* (Munich, 1996).

67. See Woodman–Martin (1996), 114–18.

68. See Woodman–Martin (1996), 168–72.

69. On rumour in Tacitus see I. Shatzman, *Latomus* 33 (1974), 549–78.

70. See EJ, pp. 41 and 49.

71. See Woodman–Martin (1996), 68–9, 217–18.

72. For other cases of displacement see Ginsburg (1981), 21–2, 55–72, although in general she believes that Tacitus followed the chronological order of events (55). A good example is Arminius' obituary at *A.* 2.88.2–3, which on Tacitus' own evidence is seemingly placed two years before the man actually died (see Goodyear (1981), 447–8).

73. The words are those of D. C. A. Shotter, *Tacitus: Annals IV* (Warminster, 1989), 5.

74. For this view see Woodman–Martin (1996), 70 and n. 1, who discuss the whole problem of dating on pp. 67–77.

75. Purcell (1993), 141; also above, p. 4.

76. For this inference see Woodman–Martin (1996), 70–1 and 114–16.

77. We should also take into account the fact that the speeches of some emperors, such as Tiberius (cf. *A.* 1.81.1, 2.63.3), were published. That Tacitus reserves a special vocabulary for his Tiberian speeches is argued by Syme (1958), 700–3 and N. P. Miller, 'Tiberius speaks', *AJP* 89 (1968), 1–19; but whether such vocabulary is authentically Tiberian cannot be proved. On the general issue see J. N. Adams, 'The vocabulary of the speeches in Tacitus' historical works', *BICS* 20 (1973), 124–44, whose position is more sceptical than those of Syme and Miller.

78. On this see A. J. Woodman, 'Contemporary history in the classical world', *Contemporary History: Practice and Method* (ed. A. Seldon, Oxford, 1988), 157–8.

79. 'public record' is a translation of *publica acta*, a phrase which recurs at *Ep.* 5.13.8 (and in Tacitus at *A.* 12.24.2) and is taken to refer to the *acta diurna* or 'daily gazette': this contained a wide variety of information (B. Baldwin, 'The *acta diurna*', *Chiron* 9 (1979), 189–203) and is referred to by Tacitus himself at *A.* 3.3.2, 13.31.1, 16.22.3. It is arguably striking that Pliny makes no assumption that Tacitus will have read of the episode in the *acta senatus*.

80. See J. Ginsburg, '*In maiores certamina*: past and present in the Annals', *TTT*, 96–103, and 'Speech and allusion in Tacitus, *Annals* 3.49–51 and 14.48–49', *AJP* 107 (1986), 525–41 respectively.

81. For a narrative example of intertextual *inventio* see Martin–Woodman (1997), 206–7, where it is argued that *A.* 4.46–51 (war in Thrace) is indebted jointly to Sall. *H.* 2.87=69 and Caes. *BG* 7.69–90. Note also e.g. E. Keitel, 'The function of the Livian reminiscences at Tacitus, *Histories* 4.58.6 and 62', *CJ* 87 (1992), 327–37.

82. For Tacitean innuendo see I. S. Ryberg, *TAPA* 73 (1942), 383–404, D. Sullivan, *CJ* 71 (1975/76), 312–36, D. Whitehead, *Latomus* 38 (1979), 474–95, R. Develin, *Antichthon* 17 (1983), 64–95.

83. In general on this topic see Walker (1952).

84. Syme (1958), 429. It has been claimed that 'the tyrants depicted by Tacitus were all

himself' (Miguel de Unamuno, quoted by L. Gossman, *Between History and Literature* (Cambridge, Ma./London, 1990), 247).

85. For these and other standard elements of biographical writing see F. Leo, *Die griechisch-römische Biographie* (Leipzig, 1901), 180–2.

86. The 'enslavement' (*seruiendum*) is to be taken as Tiberius', not as that of the Roman people collectively.

87. See e.g. Goodyear (1972), 37–40, Martin (1994), 105–6. Note also T. J. Luce, 'Tacitus' conception of historical change', in *PP*, 152–7.

88. C. Gill, 'The question of character-development: Plutarch and Tacitus', *CQ* 33 (1983), 469–87, esp. 481–7.

89. A. R. Hands, '*Postremo Suo tantum ingenio utebatur*', *CQ* 24 (1974), 312–17, esp. 316–17.

90. For the interpretation which follows see A. J. Woodman, 'Tacitus' obituary of Tiberius', *CQ* 39 (1989), 197–205.

91. For Germanicus and Drusus jointly, described as the 'New Dioscuri' on an inscription from Ephesus (*SEG* 4.515), see Strabo 6.4.2 (for Germanicus alone note Suet. *Tib.* 25.3); for Livia see Dio 57.12.2–6; for Sejanus see Vell. 127.3, 128.4, Dio 57.19.7, 58.4.3.

92. Sejanus is not mentioned in the introductory sketch, for the simple reason that, when Germanicus and Drusus were alive, his rise to prominence could not have been foreseen by contemporaries.

93. That *ingenio uti* can have this meaning is shown by *H.* 1.90.2 *ut in consiliis militiae Suetonio Paulino et Mario Celso, ita in rebus urbanis Galeri Trachali ingenio Othonem uti credebatur.* If that is the correct meaning at *A.* 6.51.3, it follows that Tacitus is there making no reference at all to 'fixed character' and that his references elsewhere to Tiberius' (dis)simulation are to be explained as characteristics of the typical tyrant figure.

94. For the interpretation which follows see A. J. Woodman, 'A death in the first act', *PLLS* 8 (1995), 257–73.

95. On the key significance of this moment see Woodman–Martin (1996), 428–9.

96. For the parallel careers of Germanicus and Drusus see B. Levick, 'Drusus Caesar and the adoptions of A.D. 4', *Latomus* 25 (1966), 239–44; Woodman–Martin (1996), 1–5. See also above, n. 91.

97. See Pelling, 'Tacitus and Germanicus', *TTT*, 59–85, esp. 78–81.

98. The moment is vividly captured in the newly discovered senatorial decree concerning Cn. Piso (above, n. 66), lines 126–30: '[the senate] earnestly asked and sought that, with reference to the concern which he had once shared between his two sons, he should transfer it to the one he still had, and the senate hoped that he who survived would be a greater concern to the immortal gods to the extent that they understood better that all future hope for his father's post on behalf of the state was placed in one man'.

99. See Martin–Woodman (1997), 90.

100. On the various devices which emphasize both the break at the start of *A.* 4 and the fact that A.D. 23 represents a turning-point see Martin–Woodman (1997), 14.

101. A. D. Heinrichs, *Sejan und das Schicksal Roms in den Annalen des Tacitus* (Diss. Marburg/Lahn, 1976).

102. On Livia see N. Purcell, 'Livia and the womanhood of Rome', *PCPS* 32 (1986), 78–105.

103. Cf. Liv. 21.43.4 *Alpes urgent.*

104. Cf. Lucr. 2.263–5 *patefactis tempore puncto / carceribus non posse tamen prorumpere equorum / uim cupidam* ('with the traps opened at a sudden moment, the eager crowd of horses still cannot charge ahead'). For Tacitus' metaphors see e.g. Walker (1952), 62–6, Martin–Woodman (1997), 22.

105. See e.g. Goodyear (1970), 29, (1972), 27, Martin (1994), 126.

106. Modern texts place commas round the clause *quod . . . reor* (see quotation).

107. See T. J. Luce, 'Tacitus on "History's Highest Function"', *ANRW* 2.33.4.2904–27, esp. 2907–14 (1991).

108. For this motif see e.g. Herkommer (1968), 164–71.

109. For this interpretation see A. J. Woodman, *Mus. Helv.* 52 (1995), 111–26.

110. Pliny's letter to Caninius Rufus, who plans to write an epic poem on Trajan's Dacian war, is relevant to historiography (*Ep.* 8.4.2 'you will tell of new rivers discharging over the land, and new bridges thrown over the rivers'). Tacitus duly writes (*A.* 15.9.1): 'Meanwhile Corbulo

occupied the Euphrates' bank, which he had never neglected, with more frequent garrisons; and, to prevent the enemy squadrons from impeding the throwing over of a bridge (for already they were flying across the surrounding plains in a great display), he deployed across the stream ships which were outstanding in size, connected by beams and augmented with turrets; and with catapults and ballistae he drove back the barbarians' (complete with a full epic hexameter in the parenthesis: *subiectis campis magna specie uolitabant*).

111. There is an excellent analysis of this narrative by K. Gilmartin, 'Corbulo's campaigns in the East. An analysis of Tacitus' account', *Historia* 22 (1973), 604–26. For the allusions to Book 9 of Livy (the Caudine Forks, also alluded to in the *Histories*: above, n. 81), see Woodman in *AA*, 184.

112. See A. J. Woodman, 'Nero's alien capital: Tacitus as paradoxographer', in *AA*, 173–88. Paradoxography is a narrative sub-genre which tells of wonders, miracles etc.: see Gabba (1981).

113. See A. J. Woodman, 'Amateur dramatics at the court of Nero', in *TTT*, 104–28; for Nero as *scaenicus imperator* see Plin. *Pan.* 46.4. For comedy in the Claudian books (11 and 12) see S. K. Dickison, 'Claudius: Saturnalicius Princeps', *Latomus* 36 (1977), 634–47.

114. The standard work is G. Sörbom, *Variatio Sermonis Tacitei* (Uppsala, 1935); note also R. H. Martin, 'Variatio and the development of Tacitus' style', *Eranos* 51 (1953), 89–96.

115. This phenomenon is studied by A. Kohl, *Der Satznachtrag bei Tacitus* (Diss. Würzburg, 1959), with special reference to *H.* 1, *A.* 1 and 13. Note also Chausserie-Laprée (1969).

116. For Tacitus' syntax see H. Furneaux, *The Annals of Tacitus* (Oxford, ²1896), 1.42–63; for his language, J. N. Adams, 'The language of the later books of Tacitus' *Annals*', *CQ* 22 (1972), 350–73. In general Syme (1958), 340–52 and 711–45, F. R. D. Goodyear, 'Development of language and style in the *Annals* of Tacitus', *JRS* 58 (1968), 22–31.

117. Syme (1958), 342–4; for 'misuse', for which the technical terms are *abusio* or *catachresis*, see e.g. Woodman–Martin (1996), 132.

118. Reversal of names is not peculiar to Tacitus (see Goodyear (1972), 148) but is esp. characteristic of him.

119. *Memoirs of the Prince de Talleyrand* (ed. Duc De Broglie, trans. R. L. De Beaufort, New York/London, 1891), 332.

120. Walker (1952), 241 and n. 1, Martin (1994), 225.

121. See e.g. Gay (1974), 21–34 (esp. 25–6). Gibbon's relationship to Tacitus has been qualified in various ways by P. Cartledge, 'The "Tacitism" of Edward Gibbon', *Mediterranean Historical Review* 4 (1989), 251–70; see also the same author's 'Vindicating Gibbon's good faith', *Hermathena* 158 (1995), 133–47, which incorporates a discussion of some basic historiographical issues.

122. Clive (1987), 106, cf. 49. Tacitus himself said that 'disparagement and malice are received favourably' (*H.* 1.1.2).

123. For a discussion of the relationship between the *Dialogus* and Tacitus' historiography see C. O. Brink, 'History in the "Dialogus de Oratoribus" and Tacitus the historian', *Hermes* 121 (1993), 335–49.

124. Clive (1987), 252, quoting Macaulay's sister, Margaret.

125. Tulloch (1988), 5–6.

126. Respectively Tulloch (1988), 95, Clive (1989), 83, Tulloch (1988), 81.

127. Tacitus refers to Augustus' *Res Gestae* 8.5 'I restored many examples of our ancestors which were already fading from our period, and I myself handed on examples of many things to be imitated by posterity'.

128. i.e. whether or not posterity does imitate them, something which Tacitus naturally cannot foresee.

129. Syme (1958), 339, 565, 624 n. 3.

APPENDIX

Latin historians often made statements, especially in prefaces, about their own authorial activity: see Herkommer (1968) and T. Janson, *Latin Prose Prefaces* (Stockholm, 1964). For a full and up-to-date discussion of these and other programmatic statements see J. M. Marincola, *Authority and Tradition in Ancient Historiography* (Cambridge, 1997). The second-century A.D. Greek writer Lucian produced a short work entitled 'How to write history' (*De historia conscribenda*): in German there is a study by G. Avenarius, *Lukians Schrift zur Geschichtsschreibung* (Meisenheim am Glan, 1956) and a commentary by H. Homeyer (Munich, 1965).

Early historians

The fragments are collected in the first volume of H. Peter, *Historicorum Romanorum Reliquiae* (Leipzig [2]1914, repr. 1993); all our citations are from this edition (so e.g. Cato 86P). The best discussion is now Oakley (1997), esp. 72–104, with further refs., but note also Badian (1966) and Rawson (1991), 245–71 on 'The first Latin annalists' (orig. published 1976; the volume contains Rawson's other important studies on, or relating to, Roman historiography). Recent work on individual historians includes W. Herrmann, *Die Historien des Coelius Antipater* (Meisenheim am Glan, 1979); Rawson (1991), 363–88 on 'L. Cornelius Sisenna and the early first century B.C.' (orig. published 1979); G. Forsythe, 'Some notes on the history of Cassius Hemina', *Phoenix* 44 (1990), 326–44; Forsythe (1994) on Piso; C. Santini, ed., *I frammenti di L. Cassio Emina* (Pisa, 1995); and M. Chassignet, ed., *L'Annalistique romaine*: Tome 1, *Les Annales des pontifes et l'annalistique ancienne (fragments)* (Budé, 1996).

Sallust

There is a new edition of Sallust's two monographs, together with some of the fragments of the *Historiae*, by L. D. Reynolds (OCT, 1991); A. Kurfess' edition (Teubner, [3]1957) remains useful for its collection of *testimonia* on Sallust's life and reception (pp. xxii–xxxi). An exhaustive commentary on *BC* was produced by K. Vretska (2 vols., Heidelberg, 1976); P. McGushin's commentary (1977) was boiled down once for use in schools and universities (Bristol, [2]1987), then again for those reading

Sallust in translation (Bristol, 1987). The most recent commentary is that by J. T. Ramsey (Chico, 1984). As for the *BJ*, there are substantial commentaries by E. Koestermann (Heidelberg, 1971) and G. M. Paul (1984); finally, there exist numerous older school commentaries on both *BC* and *BJ*, many of them containing helpful information but most now out of print.

The standard edition of the fragments of the *Historiae* remains that of B. Maurenbrecher (Stuttgart 1893), but there is now a useful translation and commentary by P. McGushin (2 vols., 1992–94). Since the latter re-numbers many of the fragments, we refer to them in the form '1.4 = 3' (Maurenbrecher and McGushin in that order); translations from the *Historiae* are taken from McGushin, with modifications. There is also an Italian commentary on the speeches and letters by E. Pasoli, *Le* Historiae *e le opere minori di Sallustio* (Bologna, 1967).

A good, general book in English on Sallust is badly needed, although there is much characteristic perception and apt comment in Syme (1964); note also W. Steidle, *Sallusts historische Monographien* (Wiesbaden, 1958), Earl (1961), A. La Penna, *Sallustio e la 'rivoluzione' romana* (Milan, 1968) and E. Tiffou, *Essai sur la pensée morale de Salluste à la lumière de ses prologues* (Paris, 1974). A.D. Leeman, *A Systematical Bibliography of Sallust* (Leiden, ²1965) is now out of date, but note C. Becker, *ANRW* 1.3.720–54 (1973).

We have not discussed the two works attributed to Sallust but generally deemed to be spurious (the *Epistulae ad Caesarem senem de re publica* and the *In M. Tullium Ciceronem oratio*, both included as the Appendix Sallustiana in Reynolds' OCT, together with the equally spurious Ciceronian *In C. Sallustium Crispum oratio*): see Syme (1964), 313–51.

Livy

No modern critical edition of the whole of the surviving *Ab urbe condita* exists, but the Loeb (14 vols., various edd., Cambridge, Ma./London, 1919–67) contains the whole text and a full index. There are OCTs of all but the fifth decade (1–5, ed. R. M. Ogilvie, 1974; 6–10, and 21–5, ed. R. S. Conway and C. F. Walters, 1912–28; 26–30, ed. S. K. Johnson and R. S. Conway, ²1953; 31–5, ed. A. H. McDonald, 1965), and P. G. Walsh is preparing a text of 36–40; all the books have been edited by Teubner (edd. W. Weissenborn, M. Müller, and W. Heraeus, 1891–1914; modern editions of 21–2 and 23–4, ed. T. A. Dorey, 1971–7; 26–7, ed. P. G. Walsh, ²1989; 31–45, ed. J. Briscoe, 1985–91); in the Budé series, 1–8, 21, 25–6, 28–9, 31, 36–45 have so far appeared (various edd., 1947–). There is a commentary on the whole by W. Weissenborn and H. J. Müller (revised by O. Rossbach, Berlin 1880–1910, repr. 1962) and on individual books by J. Heurgon (1, Paris, [2]1970), R. M. Ogilvie (1–5, Oxford, [2]1970), C. S. Kraus (6, 1994), S. P. Oakley (6, 1997; 7–10 forthcoming), P. G. Walsh (21, London, 1973, repr. Bristol, 1991; 36–40, Warminster, 1990–96), T. A. Dorey and C. W. F. Lydall (29, Havant, 1968; 33, London, 1972), J. Briscoe (31–7, Oxford, 1973–81). As with Sallust and Tacitus, many older school editions, of varying quality, exist; noteworthy is W. B. Anderson on Book 9 (Cambridge, [3]1928). The *periochae* (late-antique summaries of all but Books 136–7) were edited separately by O. Rossbach (Leipzig, 1910); they and the fragments are accessible in Loeb, Budé, and Teubner editions.

There are several general studies of Livy, though they differ in specific focus: Walsh (1961) and Luce (1977) are the best known in English; Walsh also wrote an earlier *Greece & Rome* New Survey on Livy (1974), and there are various essays collected in T. A. Dorey, ed., *Livy* (London, 1971). In German, the work of E. Burck is important (esp. *Die Erzählungskunst des T. Livius*, Berlin, [2]1964; *Einführung in die dritte Dekade des Livius*, Heidelberg, [2]1962; and *Das Geschichtswerk des Titus Livius*, Heidelberg, 1992); also of interest is L. Catin, *En lisant Tite-Live* (Paris, 1944). The most recent bibliographical survey is by W. Kissel, *ANRW* 2.30.2.899–997 (1982), accompanied by a survey by J. E. Phillips of current work on the first decade (998–1057) and by H. Aili of work on Livy's language (1122–47).

First century A.D.

The fragments of the lost historians are assembled in the second volume of Peter (1906, repr. 1993: see above under 'Early historians'); for discussion see Syme (1958), 132–56, R. H. Martin, 'Tacitus and his predecessors', in *Tacitus* (ed. T. A. Dorey, London, 1969), 117–47, J. Wilkes, 'Julio-Claudian historians', *CW* 65 (1972), 177–203, and *RICH*, 140–6.

There is a recent edition of Velleius by W. S. Watt (Teubner, 1988); earlier there was J. Hellegouarc'h (Budé, 1982), who also produced a bibliographical survey in *ANRW* 2.32.1.404–36 (1984). There are commentaries by M. Elefante (Hildesheim, 1996) and (on Velleius' narrative of Caesar, Augustus, and Tiberius) by Woodman (2 vols., 1977–83), who also produced a general literary appraisal in *Empire and Aftermath: Silver Latin II* (ed. T. A. Dorey, London, 1975), 1–25; more historical is the excellent discussion by Sumner (1970), and note also C. Kuntze, *Zur Darstellung des Kaisers Tiberius und seiner Zeit bei Velleius Paterculus* (Frankfurt, 1985).

The most convenient edition of Curtius is that by J. C. Rolfe in the Loeb series (2 vols., Cambridge, Ma./London, 1946), and J. E. Atkinson has written a commentary on Books 3–7.2 (2 vols., Amsterdam 1980–94). Curtius has been translated recently by J. C. Yardley in a Penguin edition (Harmondsworth, 1984), with a useful introduction, notes and bibliography by W. Heckel. For a general appraisal see E. I. McQueen, *Latin Biography* (ed. T. A. Dorey, London, 1967), 17–43; for source-criticism see N. G. L. Hammond, *Three Historians of Alexander the Great* (Cambridge, 1983), 116–59.

Tacitus

There are editions of the *Histories* by H. Heubner (Teubner, 1978) and K. Wellesley (Teubner, 1989); the former has also produced a commentary on the whole work (5 vols., Heidelberg, 1963–82), the latter on Book 3 (Sydney, 1972). A commentary on Books 1–2 and 4–5 was written by G. E. F. Chilver (2 vols., Oxford, 1979–85).

There are editions of the *Annals* by H. Heubner (Teubner, 1983) and S. Borzsák–K. Wellesley (2 vols., Teubner, 1986–91/2). The only English commentary on the whole work remains H. Furneaux (2 vols., Oxford, ^{2}1896–1907); in German there is E. Koestermann (4 vols., Heidelberg, 1963–8). Full commentaries on Books 1–2 were written by F. R. D. Goodyear (2 vols., Cambridge, 1972–81) and on Book 3 by A. J. Woodman–R. H. Martin (1996); there are smaller commentaries on Book 1 by N. P. Miller (London, 1959, repr. 1992), Book 4 by R. H. Martin–A. J. Woodman (1997, first publ. 1989), Book 11 by H. W. Benario (Lanham, 1983), Book 14 by E. C. Woodcock (London, 1939, repr. Oxford, 1985), and Book 15 by N. P. Miller (London, 1973, repr. 1986).

The classic work on Tacitus is the two-volume study by Syme (1958); the most helpful introduction in English is Martin (1994, first publ. 1981); there is an earlier *Greece & Rome* New Survey by Goodyear (1970). There are numerous and varied contributions to Tacitean scholarship, including bibliographies and survey articles, in *ANRW* 2.33.2–5 (1990–91). Recent work in English includes *TTT*, R. Mellor, *Tacitus* (New York/London, 1993), and P. Sinclair, *Tacitus the Sententious Historian* (Pennsylvania, 1995); the most recent bibliography is by H. W. Benario, *CW* 89 (1995), 91–162.

We have not discussed Tacitus' biographical and ethnographical monographs, the *Agricola* (commentary by R. M. Ogilvie–I. Richmond, Oxford, 1967) and the *Germania* (on which there has been no decent commentary in English since that of J. G. C. Anderson, Oxford, 1938); the *Dialogus de oratoribus* is not a work of history.

Further information and bibliographical details on each of the above authors may be found in standard handbooks such as *CHCL* 2 and Conte (1994).

REFERENCES AND ABBREVIATIONS

References to most ancient authors and texts ought to be self-explanatory; Tacitus' *Annals* are abbreviated as *A.*, his *Agricola* as *Agr.* We refer to Fronto in the Loeb edition by volume and page-number.

Periodical abbreviations generally follow the system used in *L'Année philologique*. Abbreviated references to modern works are explained below in list A; in list B will be found those modern works which are referred to by author's name, date, and page-number.

A. ABBREVIATIONS

AA   *Author and Audience in Latin Literature*, edd. Tony Woodman and Jonathan Powell (Cambridge, 1992).

ANRW   *Aufstieg und Niedergang der römischen Welt*, Vols. 1– (Berlin/New York, 1972–).

CHCL 2   *Cambridge History of Classical Literature:* Vol. 2 *Latin Literature*, edd. E. J. Kenney and W. V. Clausen (Cambridge, 1982).

CIL   *Corpus Inscriptionum Latinarum* (Berlin, 1863–).

EJ   *Documents Illustrating the Reigns of Augustus and Tiberius*, edd. V. Ehrenberg and A. H. M. Jones, 2nd edn (repr.) (Oxford, 1976).

ILS   *Inscriptiones Latinae Selectae*, ed. H. Dessau (Berlin, 1892–1916).

OCT   Oxford Classical Text(s).

OLD   *Oxford Latin Dictionary*, ed. P. G. W. Glare (Oxford, 1968–82).

PP   *Past Perspectives: Studies in Greek and Roman Historical Writing*, edd. I. S. Moxon, J. D. Smart, and A. J. Woodman (Cambridge, 1986).

RICH   A. J. Woodman, *Rhetoric in Classical Historiography* (London/Sydney/Portland, 1988).

RP   R. Syme, *Roman Papers*, Vols. 1–7 (Oxford, 1979–91).

SEG   *Supplementum Epigraphicum Graecum* (Leiden, 1923–).

TTT   *Tacitus and the Tacitean Tradition*, edd. T. J. Luce and A. J. Woodman (Princeton, 1993).

B. OTHER MODERN WORKS

Badian, E. (1966): 'The Early Historians', in *Latin Historians*, ed. T. A. Dorey, 1–38 (London).

Balsdon, J. P. V. D. (1979): *Romans and Aliens* (London).

Barthes, R. (1975): *S/Z*. Eng. trans. (London).

Booth, W. C. (1983): *The Rhetoric of Fiction*. 2nd edn. (Chicago/London).

Briscoe, J. (1981): *A Commentary on Livy Books XXXIV–XXXVII* (Oxford).

Brock, R. (1995): 'Versions, "inversions" and evasions: classical historiography and the "published" speech', *Papers of the Leeds International Latin Seminar* 8.209–24.

Bucher, G. (1987 [1995]): 'The *Annales Maximi* in the light of Roman methods of keeping records', *AJAH* 12.2–61.

Chaplin, J. D. (1993): *Livy's Use of Exempla and the Lessons of the Past* (Diss. Princeton).

Chausserie-Laprée, J.-P. (1969): *L'Expression narrative chez les historiens latins* (Paris).

Clive, J. (1987): *Macaulay: the Shaping of the Historian* (Cambridge, Ma.).

—— (1989): *Not by Fact Alone. Essays on the Writing and Reading of History* (New York).

Conte, G. B. (1994): *Latin Literature: a History*. Trans. J. B. Solodow (Baltimore/London).

Cornell, T. J. (1995): *The Beginnings of Rome* (London).

de Jong, I. J. F. and Sullivan, J. P. (1994): *Modern Critical Theory and Classical Literature* (Leiden).

Earl, D. C. (1961): *The Political Thought of Sallust* (Cambridge).

—— (1965): Review of Syme (1964), *JRS* 55.232–40.

Feeney, D. C. (1994): 'Beginning Sallust's Catiline', *Prudentia* 26.139–46.

Fornara, C. W. (1983): *The Nature of History in Ancient Greece and Rome* (Berkeley/Los Angeles/London).

Forsythe, G. (1994): *The Historian L. Calpurnius Piso Frugi and the Roman Annalistic Tradition* (Lanham).

Fowler, D. P. (1989): 'First thoughts on closure', *MD* 22.75–122.

Gabba, E. (1981): 'True history and false history in classical antiquity', *JRS* 71.50–62.

Galinsky, K. (1996): *Augustan Culture* (Princeton).

Gay, P. (1974): *Style in History* (New York/London).

Ginsburg, J. (1981): *Tradition and Theme in the Annals of Tacitus* (New York).

Goodyear, F. R. D. (1970): *Tacitus. Greece & Rome* New Surveys in the Classics 4 (Oxford).

—— (1972, 1981): *The Annals of Tacitus*. Vols. 1–2 [= *Annals* 1–2] (Cambridge).

Gowers, E. (1993): *The Loaded Table* (Oxford).

Herkommer, E. (1968): *Die Topoi in den Proömien der römischen Geschichtswerke* (Diss. Tübingen).

Heubner, H. (1972): *P. Cornelius Tacitus. Die Historien. Band II: Zweites Buch* (Heidelberg).

Horsfall, N. (1981): 'Some problems of titulature in Roman literary history', *BICS* 28.103–14.

Innes, D., Hine, H., and Pelling, C., edd. (1995): *Ethics and Rhetoric* (Oxford).

Jaeger, M. (1997): *Livy's Written Rome* (Ann Arbor).

Kaster, R. A. (1995): *Suetonius De Grammaticis et Rhetoribus* (Oxford).

Koestermann, E. (1963): *Cornelius Tacitus. Annalen. Band I: Buch 1–3* (Heidelberg).

Kraus, C. S. (1994): *Livy Ab Vrbe Condita Book VI* (Cambridge).

—— (1994a): '"No second Troy": topoi and refoundation in Livy, Book V', *TAPA* 124.267–89.

Leeman, A.D. (1963): *Orationis Ratio*. 2 vols. (Amsterdam).

Levene, D. S. (1992): 'Sallust's *Jugurtha*: an "historical fragment"', *JRS* 82.53–70.

—— (1993): *Religion in Livy* (Leiden).

Luce, T. J. (1965): 'The dating of Livy's first decade', *TAPA* 96.209–40.

—— (1977): *Livy: The Composition of his History* (Princeton).

Martin, R. (1994): *Tacitus* (first publ. 1981) (London).

Martin, R. H. and Woodman, A. J. (1997): *Tacitus Annals Book IV* (first publ. 1989) (Cambridge).

McGushin, P. (1977): *C. Sallustius Crispus. Bellum Catilinae. A Commentary* (Leiden).

—— (1992, 1994): *Sallust. The Histories*. Vols. 1–2 (Oxford).

Miles, G. B. (1995): *Livy: Reconstructing Early Rome* (Ithaca/London).

Millar, F. and Segal, E., edd. (1990): *Caesar Augustus: Seven Aspects*. Corrected edn. (Oxford).

Moles, J. (1993): 'Livy's Preface', *PCPS* 39.141–68.

Oakley, S. P. (1997): *A Commentary on Livy: Books VI–X.* Vol. 1: *Introduction and Book VI* (Oxford).

Ogilvie, R. M. (1970): *A Commentary on Livy Books 1–5.* 2nd edn. (Oxford).

Paul, G. M. (1982): 'Urbs capta: sketch of an ancient literary motif', *Phoenix* 36.144–55.

—— (1984): *A Historical Commentary on Sallust's Bellum Jugurthinum* (Liverpool).

Pearson, L. (1939): *The Early Historians of Ionia* (Oxford).

Plass, P. (1988): *Wit and the Writing of History* (Madison/London).

Pomeroy, A. J. (1991): *The Appropriate Comment: Death Notices in the Ancient Historians* (Frankfurt am Main/Bern/New York/Paris).

Purcell, N. (1993): 'Atrium Libertatis', *PBSR* 48.125–55.

Raaflaub, K. A. and Toher, M., edd. (1990): *Between Republic and Empire. Interpretations of Augustus and his Principate* (Berkeley/Los Angeles/Oxford).

Rawson, E. (1985): *Intellectual Life in the Late Roman Republic* (London).

—— (1991): *Roman Culture and Society: Collected Papers* (Oxford).

Scanlon, T. F. (1987): *Spes Frustrata. A Reading of Sallust* (Heidelberg).

—— (1988): 'Textual geography in Sallust's The war with Jugurtha', *Ramus* 17.138–75.

Sherk, R. K. (1988): *The Roman Empire: Augustus to Hadrian.* Translated Documents of Greece and Rome 6 (Cambridge).

Stadter, P. A. (1972): 'The structure of Livy's History', *Historia* 21.287–307.

Sumner, G. V. (1970): 'The truth about Velleius Paterculus: prolegomena', *HSCP* 74.257–97.

Syme, R. (1939): *The Roman Revolution* (Oxford).

—— (1958): *Tacitus* (Oxford).

—— (1964): *Sallust* (Berkeley/Los Angeles).

Thomas, R. F. (1982): *Lands and Peoples in Roman Poetry. The Ethnographical Tradition.* Camb. Philol. Soc. Suppl. 7 (Cambridge).

—— (1986): 'Virgil's *Georgics* and the art of reference', *HSCP* 90.171–98.

Tulloch, H. (1988): *Acton* (London).

Vasaly, A. (1993): *Representations: Images of the World in Ciceronian Oratory* (Berkeley/Los Angeles/London).

von Albrecht, M. (1989): *Masters of Roman Prose* (first publ. in German 1979) (Leeds).

Walbank, F. W. (1972): *Polybius* (Berkeley/Los Angeles/London).

Walker, B. (1952): *The Annals of Tacitus: a Study in the Writing of History* (Manchester).

Walsh, P. G. (1961): *Livy: His Historical Aims and Methods* (Cambridge).

—— (1990): *Livy Book XXXVI* (Warminster).

Wiseman, T. P. (1971): *New Men in the Roman Senate 139 B.C.–A.D. 14* (Oxford).

—— (1979): *Clio's Cosmetics* (Leicester).

—— (1987): *Roman Studies: Literary and Historical* (Liverpool).

Woodman, A. J. (1975): 'Questions of date, genre and style in Velleius: some literary answers', *CQ* 25.272–306.

—— (1977): *Velleius Paterculus: The Tiberian Narrative* (Cambridge).

—— (1983): *Velleius Paterculus: The Caesarian and Augustan Narrative* (Cambridge).

Woodman, A. J. and Martin R. H. (1996): *The Annals of Tacitus. Book 3* (Cambridge).

ABOUT THE AUTHORS

C. S. Kraus has taught at New York University in Manhattan and is now Lecturer in Greek and Latin at University College London. She reviews widely in the field of Roman studies, and is a contributing editor of the *Bryn Mawr Classical Review* and a correspondent of *Histos*. She has published a commentary on Livy, *Ab Urbe Condita* 6 in the series Cambridge Greek and Latin Classics (1994), and is working on another on Caesar, *De Bello Gallico* 7. She has written articles on Roman historiography and on Greek tragic narrative, and is editing a volume of papers on ancient historiography (including studies of Chinese, Near-Eastern, Biblical, and Greco-Roman historical narratives), to be published by E. J. Brill in 1998.

A. J. Woodman is Professor of Latin at the University of Durham. Previously he held appointments at the Universities of Leeds and Newcastle, and in 1989–90 was Visiting Professor at Princeton University. He is author of two volumes of commentary on Velleius Paterculus (Cambridge, 1977 and 1983) and of *Rhetoric in Classical Historiography* (London, 1988). He has co-edited several volumes of essays published by Cambridge University Press: *Quality and Pleasure in Latin Poetry* (1974), *Creative Imitation and Latin Literature* (1979), *Poetry and Politics in the Age of Augustus* (1984), *Past Perspectives: Studies in Greek and Roman Historical Writing* (1986), and *Author and Audience in Latin Literature* (1992). With T. J. Luce he edited *Tacitus and the Tacitean Tradition* (Princeton, 1993), and with R. H. Martin he has produced editions of, and commentaries on, two books of Tacitus' *Annals*: Book 3 in the series Cambridge Classical Texts and Commentaries (1996), and Book 4 in the series Cambridge Greek and Latin Classics (1989, repr. 1994 and 1997).

INDEX